OCT. 08

Test Results for Mobile Device Acquisition Tool:
Micro Systemation .XRY 3.6

NCJ 224148

David W. Hagy
Director, National Institute of Justice

This report was prepared for the National Institute of Justice, U.S. Department of Justice, by the Office of Law Enforcement Standards of the National Institute of Standards and Technology under Interagency Agreement 2003–IJ–R–029.

The National Institute of Justice is a component of the Office of Justice Programs, which also includes the Bureau of Justice Assistance, the Bureau of Justice Statistics, the Office of Juvenile Justice and Delinquency Prevention, and the Office for Victims of Crime.

May 2008

Test Results for Mobile Device Acquisition Tool:
Micro Systemation .XRY 3.6

**National Institute of
Standards and Technology**
U.S. Department of Commerce

Contents

Introduction

The Computer Forensics Tool Testing (CFTT) program is a joint project of the National Institute of Justice (NIJ), the research and development organization of the U.S. Department of Justice, and the National Institute of Standards and Technology's (NIST's) Office of Law Enforcement Standards (OLES) and Information Technology Laboratory. CFTT is supported by other organizations, including the Federal Bureau of Investigation , the U.S. Department of Defense Cyber Crime Center, U.S. Internal Revenue Service Criminal Investigation Division Electronic Crimes Program, and the U.S. Department of Homeland Security's Bureau of Immigration and Customs Enforcement, U.S. Customs and Border Protection and U.S. Secret Service. The objective of the CFTT program is to provide measurable assurance to practitioners, researchers, and other applicable users that the tools used in computer forensics investigations provide accurate results. Accomplishing this requires the development of specifications and test methods for computer forensics tools and subsequent testing of specific tools against those specifications.

Test results provide the information necessary for developers to improve tools, users to make informed choices, and the legal community and others to understand the tools' capabilities. This approach to testing computer forensic tools is based on well-recognized methodologies for conformance and quality testing. The specifications and test methods are posted on the CFTT Web site (http://www.cftt.nist.gov/) for review and comment by the computer forensics community.

This document reports the results from testing Micro Systemation .XRY, version 3.6, against the *GSM Mobile Device and Associated Media Tool Specification and Test Plan Version 1.1,* available at the CFTT Web site (http://www.cftt.nist.gov/GSM-Mobile-Device-and-Associated-Media-Tool-Specification-and-Test-Plan.pdf). Collected data packets (sent and received data transmissions) for mobile device internal memory acquisitions and SIM internal memory acquisitions, captured via a port monitoring utility, are posted at www.cftt.nist.gov/mobile_devices.htm.

Test results from other software packages and the CFTT tool methodology can be found on NIJ's computer forensics tool testing Web page, http://www.ojp.usdoj.gov/nij/topics/technology/electronic-crime/cftt.htm.

Test Results for Mobile Device Data Acquisition Tool

Tool Tested:	Micro Systemation .XRY
Version:	3.6
Run Environments:	Windows XP Service Pack 2
Supplier:	Micro Systemation
Address:	Rasundavagen 1–3
	108 68 Solna
	Sweden
Tel:	+46 (0)8–739 02 70
Fax:	+46 (0)8–730 01 70
WWW:	http://www.msab.com

1 Results Summary

Except for the following test cases (CFT–IM–05, CFT–IM–06), the tested tool acquired all supported data objects completely and accurately from the selected test mobile devices and associated media (i.e., Nokia 6101, T-Mobile SIM, Motorola RAZR V3, AT&T SIM). The exceptions are the following:

1. The MSISDN was not reported for the Nokia 6101 after a successful internal memory acquisition. (CFT–IM–05: Nokia 6101)
2. Maximum length Notes created on the Nokia 6101 were truncated preventing the entire message to be acquired. The tool reports a maximum of 184 characters within a Note. (CFT–IM–06: Nokia 6101)

2 Test Case Selection

Not all test cases or test assertions are appropriate for all tools. In addition to the base test cases, each remaining test case is linked to optional tool features needed for the test case. If a given tool implements a given feature then the test cases linked to that feature are run. Table 1 lists the features available in Micro Systemation .XRY and the linked test cases. Table 2 lists the features not available in Micro Systemation .XRY and the linked test cases.

Table 1 Selected Test Cases

Supported Optional Feature	Cases selected for execution
Base Cases	CFT–IM–(01–10), CFT–SIM–(01–10)
Acquire mobile device internal memory and review data via supported generated report formats	CFT–IMO–01
Acquire mobile device internal memory and review reported data via the preview pane	CFT–IMO–02
Acquire mobile device internal memory and compare reported data via the preview pane and supported generated report formats	CFT–IMO–03
After a successful mobile device internal memory acquisition, alter the case file via third party means and attempt to reopen the case	CFT–IMO–04
Create a SIM access card via vendor documentation	CFT–IMO–07
Acquire mobile device internal memory and review generated log files	CFT–IMO–08
Acquire mobile device internal memory and review data containing foreign language characters	CFT–IMO–09
Acquire mobile device internal memory and review hash values for vendor supported data objects	CFT–IMO–11
Acquire SIM internal memory and review acquired data via supported generated report formats	CFT–SIMO–01
Acquire SIM internal memory and review acquired data via the preview pane	CFT–SIMO–02
Acquire SIM internal memory and compare acquired data via the preview pane and supported generated reports	CFT–SIMO–03
After a successful SIM internal memory acquisition, alter the case file via third party means and attempt to reopen the case	CFT–SIMO–04

Acquire SIM internal memory and review reports for recoverable deleted data	CFT–SIMO–05
Acquire SIM internal memory and review generated log files	CFT–SIMO–06
Acquire SIM internal memory and review data containing foreign language characters	CFT–SIMO–07
Begin acquisition on a PIN protected SIM to determine if the tool provides an accurate count of the remaining number of PIN attempts and if the PIN attempts are decremented when entering an incorrect value	CFT–SIMO–08
Begin acquisition on a SIM whose PIN attempts have been exhausted to determine if the tool provides an accurate count of the remaining number of PUK attempts and if the PUK attempts are decremented when entering an incorrect value	CFT–SIMO–09

Table 2 Omitted Test Cases

Unsupported Optional Feature	Cases omitted (not executed)
Perform a physical acquisition and review data output for readability	CFT–IMO–05
Perform a physical acquisition and review reports for recoverable deleted data	CFT–IMO–06
Perform a stand-alone mobile device internal memory acquisition and review the status flags for text messages present on the SIM	CFT–IMO–10
Acquire mobile device internal memory and review the overall case file hash	CFT–IMO–12
Acquire SIM internal memory and review hash values for vendor supported data objects	CFT–SIMO–10
Acquire SIM internal memory and review the overall case file hash	CFT–SIMO–11

Some test cases have variant forms to accommodate parameters within test assertions. These variations cover the acquisition interface type (i.e., Bluetooth, Infrared).

The following source mobile device acquisition interfaces were tested: cable and Bluetooth for the Motorola RAZR V3, cable and IrDA for the Nokia 6101, and Micro Systemation's USB SIM reader for internal memory SIM acquisitions.

3 Results by Test Assertion

Table 3 summarizes the test results by assertion. The column labeled **Assertion** gives the text of each assertion. The column labeled **Tests** gives the number of test cases that use the given assertion. The column labeled **Anomaly** gives the section number in this report where the anomaly is discussed.

Table 3 Assertions Tested

Assertions Tested	Tests	Anomaly
A_IM–01 If a cellular forensic tool provides support for connectivity of the target device then the tool shall successfully recognize the target device via all vendor supported interfaces (e.g., cable, Bluetooth, IrDA).	9	
A_IM–02 If a cellular forensic tool attempts to connect to a nonsupported device then the tool shall have the ability to identify that the device is not supported.	1	
A_IM–03 If a cellular forensic tool encounters disengagement between the device and application then the application shall notify the user that connectivity has been disrupted.	1	
A_IM–04 If a cellular forensic tool successfully completes acquisition of the target device then the tool shall have the ability to present acquired data elements in a human-readable format via either a preview pane or generated report.	7	
A_IM–05 If a cellular forensic tool successfully completes acquisition of the target device then subscriber related information shall be presented in a human-readable format without modification.	1	3.1
A_IM–06 If a cellular forensic tool successfully completes acquisition of the target device then equipment related information shall be presented in a human-readable format without modification.	1	
A_IM–07 If a cellular forensic tool successfully completes acquisition of the target device then all known address book entries shall be presented in a human-readable format without modification.	1	
A_IM–08 If a cellular forensic tool successfully completes acquisition of the target device then all known maximum length address book entries shall be presented in a human-readable format without modification.	1	
A_IM–09 If a cellular forensic tool successfully completes acquisition of the target device then all known address book entries containing special characters shall be presented in a human-readable format without modification.	1	
A_IM–10 If a cellular forensic tool successfully completes acquisition of the target device then all known address book entries containing blank names shall be presented in a human-readable format without modification.	1	
A_IM–11 If a cellular forensic tool successfully completes acquisition of the target device then all known email addresses associated with	1	

address book entries shall be presented in a human-readable format without modification.		
A_IM–12 If a cellular forensic tool successfully completes acquisition of the target device then all known graphics associated with address book entries shall be presented in a human-readable format without modification.	1	
A_IM–13 If a cellular forensic tool successfully completes acquisition of the target device then all known datebook, calendar, note entries shall be presented in a human-readable format without modification.	1	
A_IM–14 If a cellular forensic tool successfully completes acquisition of the target device then all maximum length datebook, calendar, note entries shall be presented in a human-readable format without modification.	1	3.2
A_IM–15 If a cellular forensic tool successfully completes acquisition of the target device then all call logs (incoming/outgoing) shall be presented in a human-readable format without modification.	1	
A_IM–16 If a cellular forensic tool successfully completes acquisition of the target device then all text messages (i.e., SMS, EMS) messages shall be presented in a human-readable format without modification.	1	
A_IM–17 If a cellular forensic tool successfully completes acquisition of the target device then all MMS messages and associated audio shall be presented properly without modification.	1	
A_IM–18 If a cellular forensic tool successfully completes acquisition of the target device then all MMS messages and associated images shall be presented properly without modification.	1	
A_IM–19 If a cellular forensic tool successfully completes acquisition of the target device then all MMS messages and associated video shall be presented properly without modification.	1	
A_IM–20 If a cellular forensic tool successfully completes acquisition of the target device then all stand-alone audio files shall be playable via either an internal application or suggested third-party application without modification.	1	
A_IM–21 If a cellular forensic tool successfully completes acquisition of the target device then all stand-alone image files shall be viewable via either an internal application or suggested third-party application without modification.	1	
A_IM–22 If a cellular forensic tool successfully completes acquisition of the target device then all stand-alone video files shall be viewable via either an internal application or suggested third-party application without modification.	1	
A_SIM–23 If a cellular forensic tool provides support for connectivity of the target SIM then the tool shall successfully recognize the target SIM via all vendor supported interfaces (e.g., PC/SC reader, proprietary reader).	9	
A_SIM–24 If a cellular forensic tool attempts to connect to a nonsupported SIM then the tool shall have the ability to identify that the	1	

SIM is not supported.		
A_SIM–25 If a cellular forensic tool encounters disengagement between the SIM reader and application then the application shall notify the user that connectivity has been disrupted.	1	
A_SIM–26 If the SIM is password protected then the cellular forensic tool shall provide the examiner with the opportunity to input the PIN before acquisition.	1	
A_SIM–27 If a cellular forensic tool successfully completes acquisition of the target SIM then the tool shall have the ability to present acquired data in a human-readable format via either preview pane or generated report.	6	
A_SIM–28 If a cellular forensic tool successfully completes acquisition of the target SIM then the SPN shall be presented in a human-readable format without modification.	1	
A_SIM–29 If a cellular forensic tool successfully completes acquisition of the target SIM then the ICCID shall be presented in a human-readable format without modification.	1	
A_SIM–30 If a cellular forensic tool successfully completes acquisition of the target SIM then the IMSI shall be presented in a human-readable format without modification.	1	
A_SIM–31 If a cellular forensic tool successfully completes acquisition of the target SIM then the MSISDN shall be presented in a human-readable format without modification.	1	
A_SIM–32 If a cellular forensic tool successfully completes acquisition of the target SIM then all Abbreviated Dialing Numbers (ADN) shall be presented in a human-readable format without modification.	1	
A_SIM–33 If a cellular forensic tool successfully completes acquisition of the target SIM then all Last Numbers Dialed (LND) shall be presented in a human-readable format without modification.	1	
A_SIM–34 If a cellular forensic tool successfully completes acquisition of the target SIM then all SMS text messages shall be presented in a human-readable format without modification.	1	
A_SIM–35 If a cellular forensic tool successfully completes acquisition of the target SIM then all EMS text messages shall be presented in a human-readable format without modification.	1	
A_SIM–36 If a cellular forensic tool successfully completes acquisition of the target SIM then all location related data (i.e., LOCI) shall be presented in a human-readable format without modification.	1	
A_SIM–37 If a cellular forensic tool successfully completes acquisition of the target SIM then all location related data (i.e., GRPSLOCI) shall be presented in a human-readable format without modification.	1	
A_IMO–38 If a cellular forensic tool successfully completes acquisition of the target device then the tool shall present the acquired data without modification via supported generated report formats.	8	
A_IMO–39 If a cellular forensic tool successfully completes acquisition of the target device then the tool shall present the acquired data without	8	

modification in a preview-pane view.		
A_IMO–40 If a cellular forensic tool provides a preview-pane view and a generated report of the acquired data then the reports shall maintain consistency of all reported data elements.	1	
A_IMO–41 If modification is attempted to the case file or individual data elements via third-party means then the tool shall provide protection mechanisms disallowing or reporting data modification.	1	
A_IMO–51 If the cellular forensic tool supports SIM access card creation then the card creation shall be completed without errors via manufacturer suggested protocols. Access cards characteristics should be consistent with vendor documentation.	1	
A_IMO–52 If the cellular forensic tool supports log creation then the application should present the log files outlining the acquisition process in a human-readable format.	1	
A_IMO–53 If the cellular forensic tool supports proper display of foreign language character sets then the application should present address book entries containing foreign language characters in their native format without modification.	1	
A_IMO–54 If the cellular forensic tool supports proper display of foreign language character sets then the application should present text messages containing foreign language characters in their native format without modification.	1	
A_IMO–56 If the cellular forensic tool supports hashing for individual data objects then the tool shall present the user with a hash value for each supported data object.	1	
A_SIMO–58 If a cellular forensic tool successfully completes acquisition of the target media (i.e., SIM) then the tool shall present the acquired data in a human-readable format without modification via supported generated report formats.	6	
A_SIMO–59 If a cellular forensic tool successfully completes acquisition of the SIM then the tool shall present the acquired data in a human-readable format without modification in a preview-pane view.	6	
A_SIMO–60 If a cellular forensic tool provides a preview-pane view and a generated report of the acquired data then the reports shall maintain consistency of all reported data elements.	1	
A_SIMO–61 If modification is attempted to the case file or individual data elements via third-party means then the tool shall provide protection mechanisms disallowing or reporting data modification.	1	
A_SIMO–62 If the cellular forensic tool successfully completes acquisition of the target SIM and recoverable deleted SMS messages exist then the tool shall present recoverable deleted data in a human-readable format without modification.	1	
A_SIMO–63 If the cellular forensic tool successfully completes acquisition of the target SIM and recoverable deleted EMS messages exist then the tool shall present recoverable deleted data in a human-readable format without modification.	1	

A_SIMO–64 If a cellular forensic tool supports creation of log files then the application should present the log files in a human-readable format outlining the acquisition process.	1
A_SIMO–65 If the cellular forensic tool supports proper display of foreign language character sets then the application should present abbreviated dialing numbers (ADNs) containing foreign language characters in their native format without modification.	1
A_SIMO–66 If the cellular forensic tool supports proper display of foreign language character sets then the application should present text messages containing foreign language characters in their native format without modification.	1
A_SIMO–67 If a cellular forensic tool provides the examiner with the remaining number of authentication attempts then the application should provide an accurate count of the remaining PIN attempts.	1
A_SIMO–68 If a cellular forensic tool provides the examiner with the remaining number of PUK attempts then the application should provide an accurate count of the remaining PUK attempts.	1

Table 4 lists the assertions that were not tested, usually due to the tool not supporting an optional feature.

Table 4 Assertions Not Tested

Assertions not Tested
A_IMO–42 If the cellular forensic tool supports a physical acquisition of the target device then the tool shall successfully complete the acquisition and present the data in a human-readable format.
A_IMO–43 If the cellular forensic tool supports a physical acquisition of address book entries present on the target device then the tool shall report recoverable deleted data or address book data remnants in a human-readable format.
A_IMO–44 If the cellular forensic tool supports a physical acquisition of calendar, tasks, or notes present on the target device then the tool shall report recoverable deleted calendar, tasks, or note data remnants in a human-readable format.
A_IMO–45 If the cellular forensic tool supports a physical acquisition of call logs present on the target device then the tool shall report recoverable deleted call or call log data remnants in a human-readable format.
A_IMO–46 If the cellular forensic tool supports a physical acquisition of SMS messages present on the target device then the tool shall report recoverable deleted SMS messages or SMS message data remnants in a human-readable format.
A_IMO–47 If the cellular forensic tool supports a physical acquisition of EMS messages present on the target device then the tool shall report recoverable deleted EMS messages or EMS message data remnants in a human-readable format.
A_IMO–48 If the cellular forensic tool supports a physical acquisition of audio files present on the target device then the tool shall report recoverable deleted audio data or audio file data remnants in a human-readable format.

A_IMO–49 If the cellular forensic tool supports a physical acquisition of graphic files present on the target device then the tool shall report recoverable deleted graphic file data or graphic file data remnants in a human-readable format.
A_IMO–50 If the cellular forensic tool supports a physical acquisition of video files present on the target device then the tool shall report recoverable deleted video file data or video file data remnants in a human-readable format.
A_IMO–55 If the cellular forensic tool supports stand-alone acquisition of internal memory with the SIM present, then the contents of the SIM shall not be modified during internal memory acquisition.
A_IMO–57 If the cellular forensic tool supports hashing the overall case file then the tool shall present the user with one hash value representing the entire case data.
A_SIMO–69 If the cellular forensic tool supports hashing for individual data objects then the tool shall present the user with a hash value for each supported data object.
A_SIMO–70 If the cellular forensic tool supports hashing for the overall case file then the tool shall present the user with one hash value representative of the entire case data.

3.1 Acquisition of MSISDN

.XRY does not report the MSISDN from the mobile device internal memory for the Nokia 6101 (Test Case: CFT–IM–05). However, the MSISDN is acquired and reported when acquiring the internal memory of the Motorola RAZR V3.

NOTE: XRY acquires the MSISDN by sending the AT+CNUM command to the device and echoes the response. Not all devices support this command. This number is a text field on the SIM. The number is not used to identify the user by the network, therefore can be any type of number. The MSISDN can be manipulated and report misleading information.

3.2 Acquisition of PIM Data

.XRY has the ability to acquire Personal Information Management (PIM) data e.g., Calendar, Notes, To-Do list, etc. The tool reports up to 184 characters for Notes (Test Case: CFT–IM–06). Dependent upon the mobile device's design and capabilities determines the amount of characters a created Note is capable of storing. The Nokia 6101 has the ability to create a Note containing 3000 characters. Therefore, the mobile device internal memory acquisition truncated a significant amount of PIM data present on the device.

4 Testing Environment

The tests were run in the NIST CFTT lab. This section describes the test computers available for testing.

4.1 Test Computers

One test computers was used.

Morrisy has the following configuration:

Intel® D975XBX2 Motherboard
BIOS Version BX97520J.86A.2674.2007.0315.1546
Intel® Core™2 Duo CPU 6700 @ 2.66Ghz
3.25 GB RAM
1.44 MB floppy drive
LITE-ON CD H LH52N1P
LITE-ON DVDRW LH–20A1P
2 slots for removable SATA hard disk drive
8 USB 2.0 slots
2 IEEE 1394 ports
3 IEEE 1394 ports (mini)

5 Test Results

The main item of interest for interpreting the test results is determining the conformance of the device with the test assertions. Conformance with each assertion tested by a given test case is evaluated by examining **Log File Highlights** box of the test report summary.

5.1 Test Results Report Key

A summary of the actual test results is presented in this report. The following table presents a description of each section of the test report summary.

Table 5 Test Results Report Key

Heading	Description
First Line:	Test case ID, name, and version of tool tested.
Case Summary:	Test case summary from *GSM Mobile Device and Associated Media Tool Specification and Test Plan Version 1.1.*
Assertions:	The test assertions applicable to the test case, selected from *GSM Mobile Device and Associated Media Tool Specification and Test Plan Version 1.1.*
Tester Name:	Name or initials of person executing test procedure.
Test Host:	Host computer executing the test.
Test Date:	Time and date that test was started.
Device:	Source mobile device, media (i.e., SIM).
Source Setup:	Outline of data object types populated on the device or associated media (i.e., SIM).
Log Highlights:	Information extracted from various log files to illustrate conformance or nonconformance to the test assertions.
Results	Expected and actual results for each assertion tested.
Analysis	Whether or not the expected results were achieved.

5.2 Test Details

5.2.1 CFT-IM-01 (Nokia 6101)

Test Case CFT-IM-01 Micro Systemation .XRY Version 3.6	
Case Summary:	CFT-IM-01 Acquire mobile device internal memory over supported interfaces (e.g., cable, Bluetooth, IrDA).
Assertions:	A_IM-01 If a cellular forensic tool provides support for connectivity of the target device then the tool shall successfully recognize the target device via all vendor supported interfaces (e.g., cable, Bluetooth, IrDA).
Tester Name:	rpa
Test Host:	Morrisy
Test Date:	Wed Apr 2 09:05:31 EDT 2008
Device:	Nokia 6101
Source Setup:	OS: WIN XP Interface: cable

DATA OBJECTS	DATA ELEMENTS
Address Book Entries	
	Maximum Length
	Regular Length, email, picture
	Special Character
	Blank Name
	Regular Length, Deleted email - deleted picture
	Deleted Entry
	Foreign Entry
PIM Data	
	Maximum Length
	Regular Length
	Deleted Entry
	Special Character
Call Logs	
	Missed
	Missed - Deleted
	Incoming
	Incoming - Deleted
	Outgoing
	Outgoing - Deleted
Text Messages	
	Incoming SMS - Read
	Incoming SMS - Unread
	Incoming SMS - Deleted
	Outgoing SMS
	Outgoing SMS - Deleted
	Incoming EMS - Read
	Incoming EMS - Unread
	Incoming Foreign EMS - Read
	Incoming EMS - Deleted
	Outgoing EMS
	Outgoing EMS - Deleted
MMS Messages	
	Incoming Audio
	Incoming Image
	Incoming Video
	Outgoing Audio
	Outgoing Image
	Outgoing Video
Stand-alone data files	
	Audio
	Audio - Deleted
	Image
	Image - Deleted
	Video
	Video - Deleted

Test Case CFT-IM-01 Micro Systemation .XRY Version 3.6

Log Highlights:	Created By .XRY Version 3.6 Acquisition started: Wed Apr 2 09:05:31 EDT 2008 Acquisition finished: Wed Apr 2 09:25:40 EDT 2008 Device connectivity was established via supported interface (i.e., cable, IrDA) **Notes**: IrDA acquisition reported: General Phone Information, Contacts, Calls, and Calendar entries all which were consistent with cable acquires. Bluetooth acquisition not supported.
Results:	

Assertion & Expected Result	Actual Result
A_IM-01 Device connectivity via supported interfaces.	as expected

Analysis:	Expected results achieved

5.2.2 CFT-IM-02 (Nokia 6101)

Test Case CFT-IM-02 Micro Systemation .XRY Version 3.6	
Case Summary:	CFT-IM-02 Attempt internal memory acquisition of a non-supported mobile device.
Assertions:	A_IM-02 If a cellular forensic tool attempts to connect to a non-supported device then the tool shall have the ability to identify that the device is not supported.
Tester Name:	rpa
Test Host:	Morrisy
Test Date:	Wed Apr 2 10:00:15 EDT 2008
Device:	Non-supported mobile device
Source Setup:	OS: WIN XP Interface: cable

DATA OBJECTS	DATA ELEMENTS
Address Book Entries	
	Maximum Length
	Regular Length, email, picture
	Special Character
	Blank Name
	Regular Length, Deleted email - deleted picture
	Deleted Entry
	Foreign Entry
PIM Data	
	Maximum Length
	Regular Length
	Deleted Entry
	Special Character
Call Logs	
	Missed
	Missed - Deleted
	Incoming
	Incoming - Deleted
	Outgoing
	Outgoing - Deleted
Text Messages	
	Incoming SMS - Read
	Incoming SMS - Unread
	Incoming SMS - Deleted
	Outgoing SMS
	Outgoing SMS - Deleted
	Incoming EMS - Read
	Incoming EMS - Unread
	Incoming Foreign EMS - Read
	Incoming EMS - Deleted
	Outgoing EMS
	Outgoing EMS - Deleted
MMS Messages	
	Incoming Audio
	Incoming Image
	Incoming Video
	Outgoing Audio
	Outgoing Image
	Outgoing Video
Stand-alone data files	
	Audio
	Audio - Deleted
	Image
	Image - Deleted
	Video
	Video - Deleted

Log	Created By .XRY Version 3.6

Test Case CFT-IM-02 Micro Systemation .XRY Version 3.6	
Highlights:	Acquisition started: Wed Apr 2 10:00:15 EDT 2008 Acquisition finished: Wed Apr 2 10:01:00 EDT 2008 Identification of non-supported devices was successful
Results:	

Assertion & Expected Result	Actual Result
A IM-02 Identification of non-supported devices.	as expected

Analysis:	Expected results achieved

5.2.3 CFT-IM-03 (Nokia 6101)

Test Case CFT-IM-03 Micro Systemation .XRY Version 3.6	
Case Summary:	CFT-IM-03 Begin mobile device internal memory acquisition and interrupt connectivity by interface disengagement.
Assertions:	A_IM-01 If a cellular forensic tool provides support for connectivity of the target device then the tool shall successfully recognize the target device via all vendor supported interfaces (e.g., cable, Bluetooth, IrDA). A_IM-03 If a cellular forensic tool encounters disengagement between the device and application then the application shall notify the user that connectivity has been disrupted.
Tester Name:	rpa
Test Host:	Morrisy
Test Date:	Wed Apr 2 10:03:48 EDT 2008
Device:	Nokia 6101
Source Setup:	OS: WIN XP Interface: cable

DATA OBJECTS	DATA ELEMENTS
Address Book Entries	
	Maximum Length
	Regular Length, email, picture
	Special Character
	Blank Name
	Regular Length, Deleted email - deleted picture
	Deleted Entry
	Foreign Entry
PIM Data	
	Maximum Length
	Regular Length
	Deleted Entry
	Special Character
Call Logs	
	Missed
	Missed - Deleted
	Incoming
	Incoming - Deleted
	Outgoing
	Outgoing - Deleted
Text Messages	
	Incoming SMS - Read
	Incoming SMS - Unread
	Incoming SMS - Deleted
	Outgoing SMS
	Outgoing SMS - Deleted
	Incoming EMS - Read
	Incoming EMS - Unread
	Incoming Foreign EMS - Read
	Incoming EMS - Deleted
	Outgoing EMS
	Outgoing EMS - Deleted
MMS Messages	
	Incoming Audio
	Incoming Image
	Incoming Video
	Outgoing Audio
	Outgoing Image
	Outgoing Video
Stand-alone data files	
	Audio
	Audio - Deleted
	Image
	Image - Deleted
	Video
	Video - Deleted

Test Case CFT-IM-03 Micro Systemation .XRY Version 3.6	
Log Highlights:	Created By .XRY Version 3.6 Acquisition started: Wed Apr 2 10:03:48 EDT 2008 Acquisition finished: Wed Apr 2 10:14:15 EDT 2008 Device connectivity was established via supported interface Device acquisition disruption notification was successful **Notes:** If cable is pulled from the device interface or the device is powered off the acquisition progress bar pauses until the device cable is reconnected or the phone is powered on. When the cable is pulled from the XRY hub the examiner is notified immediately.
Results:	

Assertion & Expected Result	Actual Result
A IM-01 Device connectivity via supported interfaces.	as expected
A_IM-03 Notification of device acquisition disruption.	as expected

Analysis:	Expected results achieved

5.2.4 CFT-IM-04 (Nokia 6101)

Test Case CFT-IM-04 Micro Systemation .XRY Version 3.6	
Case Summary:	CFT-IM-04 Acquire mobile device internal memory and review reported data via the preview-pane or generated reports for readability.
Assertions:	A_IM-01 If a cellular forensic tool provides support for connectivity of the target device then the tool shall successfully recognize the target device via all vendor supported interfaces (e.g., cable, Bluetooth, IrDA). A_IM-04 If a cellular forensic tool successfully completes acquisition of the target device then the tool shall have the ability to present acquired data elements in a human-readable format via either a preview-pane or generated report.
Tester Name:	rpa
Test Host:	Morrisy
Test Date:	Wed Apr 2 10:33:54 EDT 2008
Device:	Nokia_6101
Source Setup:	OS: WIN XP Interface: cable

DATA OBJECTS	DATA ELEMENTS
Address Book Entries	
	Maximum Length
	Regular Length, email, picture
	Special Character
	Blank Name
	Regular Length, Deleted email - deleted picture
	Deleted Entry
	Foreign Entry
PIM Data	
	Maximum Length
	Regular Length
	Deleted Entry
	Special Character
Call Logs	
	Missed
	Missed - Deleted
	Incoming
	Incoming - Deleted
	Outgoing
	Outgoing - Deleted
Text Messages	
	Incoming SMS - Read
	Incoming SMS - Unread
	Incoming SMS - Deleted
	Outgoing SMS
	Outgoing SMS - Deleted
	Incoming EMS - Read
	Incoming EMS - Unread
	Incoming Foreign EMS - Read
	Incoming EMS - Deleted
	Outgoing EMS
	Outgoing EMS - Deleted
MMS Messages	
	Incoming Audio
	Incoming Image
	Incoming Video
	Outgoing Audio
	Outgoing Image
	Outgoing Video
Stand-alone data files	
	Audio
	Audio - Deleted
	Image
	Image - Deleted
	Video
	Video - Deleted

Test Case CFT-IM-04 Micro Systemation .XRY Version 3.6	
Log Highlights:	Created By .XRY Version 3.6 Acquisition started: Wed Apr 2 10:33:54 EDT 2008 Acquisition finished: Wed Apr 2 10:49:26 EDT 2008 Device connectivity was established via supported interface Readability and completeness of acquired data was successful
Results:	<table><tr><td>Assertion & Expected Result</td><td>Actual Result</td></tr><tr><td>A IM-01 Device connectivity via supported interfaces.</td><td>as expected</td></tr><tr><td>A_IM-04 Readability and completeness of acquired data via supported reports.</td><td>as expected</td></tr></table>
Analysis:	Expected results achieved

5.2.5 CFT-IM-05 (Nokia 6101)

Test Case CFT-IM-05 Micro Systemation .XRY Version 3.6	
Case Summary:	CFT-IM-05 Acquire mobile device internal memory and review reported subscriber and equipment related information (i.e., IMEI, MSISDN).
Assertions:	A_IM-01 If a cellular forensic tool provides support for connectivity of the target device then the tool shall successfully recognize the target device via all vendor supported interfaces (e.g., cable, Bluetooth, IrDA). A_IM-04 If a cellular forensic tool successfully completes acquisition of the target device then the tool shall have the ability to present acquired data elements in a human-readable format via either a preview-pane or generated report. A_IM-05 If a cellular forensic tool successfully completes acquisition of the target device then subscriber related information shall be presented in a human-readable format without modification. A_IM-06 If a cellular forensic tool successfully completes acquisition of the target device then equipment related information shall be presented in a human-readable format without modification.
Tester Name:	rpa
Test Host:	Morrisy
Test Date:	Wed Apr 2 10:54:25 EDT 2008
Device:	Nokia_6101
Source Setup:	OS: WIN XP Interface: USB

DATA OBJECTS	DATA ELEMENTS
Address Book Entries	
	Maximum Length
	Regular Length, email, picture
	Special Character
	Blank Name
	Regular Length, Deleted email - deleted picture
	Deleted Entry
	Foreign Entry
PIM Data	
	Maximum Length
	Regular Length
	Deleted Entry
	Special Character
Call Logs	
	Missed
	Missed - Deleted
	Incoming
	Incoming - Deleted
	Outgoing
	Outgoing - Deleted
Text Messages	
	Incoming SMS - Read
	Incoming SMS - Unread
	Incoming SMS - Deleted
	Outgoing SMS
	Outgoing SMS - Deleted
	Incoming EMS - Read
	Incoming EMS - Unread
	Incoming Foreign EMS - Read
	Incoming EMS - Deleted
	Outgoing EMS
	Outgoing EMS - Deleted
MMS Messages	
	Incoming Audio
	Incoming Image
	Incoming Video
	Outgoing Audio
	Outgoing Image
	Outgoing Video
Stand-alone data files	

Test Case CFT-IM-05 Micro Systemation .XRY Version 3.6	
	Audio
	Audio - Deleted
	Image
	Image - Deleted
	Video
	Video - Deleted

Log Highlights:	Created By .XRY Version 3.6 Acquisition started: Wed Apr 2 10:54:25 EDT 2008 Acquisition finished: Wed Apr 2 11:12:19 EDT 2008 Device connectivity was established via supported interface Readability and completeness of acquired data was successful MSISDN was not acquired

Results:

Assertion & Expected Result	Actual Result
A_IM-01 Device connectivity via supported interfaces.	as expected
A_IM-04 Readability and completeness of acquired data via supported reports.	as expected
A_IM-05 Acquisition of MSISDN.	Not as expected
A_IM-06 Acquisition of IMEI.	as expected

Analysis:	Partial results achieved

5.2.6 CFT-IM-06 (Nokia 6101)

Test Case CFT-IM-06 Micro Systemation .XRY Version 3.6	
Case Summary:	CFT-IM-06 Acquire mobile device internal memory and review reported PIM related data.
Assertions:	A_IM-01 If a cellular forensic tool provides support for connectivity of the target device then the tool shall successfully recognize the target device via all vendor supported interfaces (e.g., cable, Bluetooth, IrDA). A_IM-04 If a cellular forensic tool successfully completes acquisition of the target device then the tool shall have the ability to present acquired data elements in a human-readable format via either a preview-pane or generated report. A_IM-07 If a cellular forensic tool successfully completes acquisition of the target device then all known address book entries shall be presented in a human-readable format without modification. A_IM-08 If a cellular forensic tool successfully completes acquisition of the target device then all known maximum length address book entries shall be presented in a human-readable format without modification. A_IM-09 If a cellular forensic tool successfully completes acquisition of the target device then all known address book entries containing special characters shall be presented in a human-readable format without modification. A_IM-10 If a cellular forensic tool successfully completes acquisition of the target device then all known address book entries containing blank names shall be presented in a human-readable format without modification. A_IM-11 If a cellular forensic tool successfully completes acquisition of the target device then all known email addresses associated with address book entries shall be presented in a human-readable format without modification. A_IM-12 If a cellular forensic tool successfully completes acquisition of the target device then all known graphics associated with address book entries shall be presented in a human-readable format without modification. A_IM-13 If a cellular forensic tool successfully completes acquisition of the target device then all known datebook, calendar, note entries shall be presented in a human-readable format without modification. A_IM-14 If a cellular forensic tool successfully completes acquisition of the target device then all maximum length datebook, calendar, note entries shall be presented in a human readable format without modification.
Tester Name:	rpa
Test Host:	Morrisy
Test Date:	Thu Apr 3 08:35:59 EDT 2008
Device:	Nokia 6101
Source Setup:	OS: WIN XP Interface: cable

DATA OBJECTS	DATA ELEMENTS
Address Book Entries	
	Maximum Length
	Regular Length, email, picture
	Special Character
	Blank Name
	Regular Length, Deleted email - deleted picture
	Deleted Entry
	Foreign Entry
PIM Data	
	Maximum Length
	Regular Length
	Deleted Entry
	Special Character
Call Logs	
	Missed
	Missed - Deleted
	Incoming
	Incoming - Deleted
	Outgoing
	Outgoing - Deleted
Text Messages	

		Incoming SMS - Read
		Incoming SMS - Unread
		Incoming SMS - Deleted
		Outgoing SMS
		Outgoing SMS - Deleted
		Incoming EMS - Read
		Incoming EMS - Unread
		Incoming Foreign EMS - Read
		Incoming EMS - Deleted
		Outgoing EMS
		Outgoing EMS - Deleted
MMS Messages		
		Incoming Audio
		Incoming Image
		Incoming Video
		Outgoing Audio
		Outgoing Image
		Outgoing Video
Stand-alone data files		
		Audio
		Audio - Deleted
		Image
		Image - Deleted
		Video
		Video - Deleted

Log Highlights:	Created By .XRY Version 3.6 Acquisition started: Thu Apr 3 08:35:59 EDT 2008 Acquisition finished: Thu Apr 3 08:52:44 EDT 2008 Device connectivity was established via supported interface Readability and completeness of acquired data was successful All address book entries were successfully acquired Basic PIM related data was acquired Partial Maximum length PIM related data was acquired **Notes:** Address book entries containing pictures were not linked directly to the corresponding name. Maximum Length Notes were truncated allowing a maximum of 184 characters.
Results:	

Assertion & Expected Result	Actual Result
A_IM-01 Device connectivity via supported interfaces.	as expected
A_IM-04 Readability and completeness of acquired data via supported reports.	as expected
A_IM-07 Acquisition of address book entries.	as expected
A_IM-08 Acquisition of maximum length address book entries.	as expected
A_IM-09 Acquisition of address book entries containing special characters.	as expected
A_IM-10 Acquisition of address book entries containing a blank name entry.	as expected
A_IM-11 Acquisition of embedded email addresses within address book entries.	as expected
A_IM-12 Acquisition of embedded graphics within address book entries.	as expected
A_IM-13 Acquisition of PIM data (i.e., datebook/calendar, notes).	as expected
A_IM-14 Acquisition of maximum length PIM data.	Not as expected

5.2.7 CFT-IM-07 (Nokia 6101)

Test Case CFT-IM-07 Micro Systemation .XRY Version 3.6	
Case Summary:	CFT-IM-07 Acquire mobile device internal memory and review reported call logs.
Assertions:	A_IM-01 If a cellular forensic tool provides support for connectivity of the target device then the tool shall successfully recognize the target device via all vendor supported interfaces (e.g., cable, Bluetooth, IrDA). A_IM-04 If a cellular forensic tool successfully completes acquisition of the target device then the tool shall have the ability to present acquired data elements in a human-readable format via either a preview-pane or generated report. A_IM-15 If a cellular forensic tool successfully completes acquisition of the target device then all call logs (incoming/outgoing) shall be presented in a human-readable format without modification.
Tester Name:	rpa
Test Host:	Morrisy
Test Date:	Thu Apr 3 09:35:35 EDT 2008
Device:	Nokia 6101
Source Setup:	OS: WIN XP Interface: cable

DATA OBJECTS	DATA ELEMENTS
Address Book Entries	
	Maximum Length
	Regular Length, email, picture
	Special Character
	Blank Name
	Regular Length, Deleted email - deleted picture
	Deleted Entry
	Foreign Entry
PIM Data	
	Maximum Length
	Regular Length
	Deleted Entry
	Special Character
Call Logs	
	Missed
	Missed - Deleted
	Incoming
	Incoming - Deleted
	Outgoing
	Outgoing - Deleted
Text Messages	
	Incoming SMS - Read
	Incoming SMS - Unread
	Incoming SMS - Deleted
	Outgoing SMS
	Outgoing SMS - Deleted
	Incoming EMS - Read
	Incoming EMS - Unread
	Incoming Foreign EMS - Read
	Incoming EMS - Deleted
	Outgoing EMS
	Outgoing EMS - Deleted
MMS Messages	
	Incoming Audio
	Incoming Image
	Incoming Video
	Outgoing Audio
	Outgoing Image
	Outgoing Video
Stand-alone data files	
	Audio
	Audio - Deleted
	Image

Test Case CFT-IM-07 Micro Systemation .XRY Version 3.6

	Image - Deleted
	Video
	Video - Deleted

Log Highlights:	Created By .XRY Version 3.6 Acquisition started: Thu Apr 3 09:35:35 EDT 2008 Acquisition finished: Thu Apr 3 09:57:33 EDT 2008 Device connectivity was established via supported interface Readability and completeness of acquired data was successful All Call Logs (incoming, outgoing) were acquired
Results:	

Assertion & Expected Result	Actual Result
A_IM-01 Device connectivity via supported interfaces.	as expected
A_IM-04 Readability and completeness of acquired data via supported reports.	as expected
A IM-15 Acquisition of call logs.	as expected

Analysis:	Expected results achieved

5.2.8 CFT-IM-08 (Nokia 6101)

Test Case CFT-IM-08 Micro Systemation .XRY Version 3.6	
Case Summary:	CFT-IM-08 Acquire mobile device internal memory and review reported text messages.
Assertions:	A_IM-01 If a cellular forensic tool provides support for connectivity of the target device then the tool shall successfully recognize the target device via all vendor supported interfaces (e.g., cable, Bluetooth, IrDA). A_IM-04 If a cellular forensic tool successfully completes acquisition of the target device then the tool shall have the ability to present acquired data elements in a human-readable format via either a preview-pane or generated report. A_IM-16 If a cellular forensic tool successfully completes acquisition of the target device then all text messages (i.e., SMS, EMS) messages shall be presented in a human-readable format without modification.
Tester Name:	rpa
Test Host:	Morrisy
Test Date:	Thu Apr 3 09:05:39 EDT 2008
Device:	Nokia 6101
Source Setup:	OS: WIN XP Interface: USB

DATA OBJECTS	DATA ELEMENTS
Address Book Entries	
	Maximum Length
	Regular Length, email, picture
	Special Character
	Blank Name
	Regular Length, Deleted email - deleted picture
	Deleted Entry
	Foreign Entry
PIM Data	
	Maximum Length
	Regular Length
	Deleted Entry
	Special Character
Call Logs	
	Missed
	Missed - Deleted
	Incoming
	Incoming - Deleted
	Outgoing
	Outgoing - Deleted
Text Messages	
	Incoming SMS - Read
	Incoming SMS - Unread
	Incoming SMS - Deleted
	Outgoing SMS
	Outgoing SMS - Deleted
	Incoming EMS - Read
	Incoming EMS - Unread
	Incoming Foreign EMS - Read
	Incoming EMS - Deleted
	Outgoing EMS
	Outgoing EMS - Deleted
MMS Messages	
	Incoming Audio
	Incoming Image
	Incoming Video
	Outgoing Audio
	Outgoing Image
	Outgoing Video
Stand-alone data files	
	Audio
	Audio - Deleted
	Image

Test Case CFT-IM-08 Micro Systemation .XRY Version 3.6		
	Image - Deleted	
	Video	
	Video - Deleted	

Log Highlights:	Created By .XRY Version 3.6 Acquisition started: Thu Apr 3 09:05:39 EDT 2008 Acquisition finished: Thu Apr 3 09:34:44 EDT 2008 Device connectivity was established via supported interface Readability and completeness of acquired data was successful ALL text messages (SMS, EMS) were acquired

Results:		
	Assertion & Expected Result	**Actual Result**
	A_IM-01 Device connectivity via supported interfaces.	as expected
	A_IM-04 Readability and completeness of acquired data via supported reports.	as expected
	A_IM-16 Acquisition of text messages.	as expected

Analysis:	Expected results achieved

5.2.9 CFT-IM-09 (Nokia 6101)

Test Case CFT-IM-09 Micro Systemation .XRY Version 3.6	
Case Summary:	CFT-IM-09 Acquire mobile device internal memory and review reported MMS multi-media related data (i.e., text, audio, graphics, video).
Assertions:	A_IM-01 If a cellular forensic tool provides support for connectivity of the target device then the tool shall successfully recognize the target device via all vendor supported interfaces (e.g., cable, Bluetooth, IrDA). A_IM-04 If a cellular forensic tool successfully completes acquisition of the target device then the tool shall have the ability to present acquired data elements in a human-readable format via either a preview-pane or generated report. A_IM-17 If a cellular forensic tool successfully completes acquisition of the target device then all MMS messages and associated audio shall be presented properly without modification. A_IM-18 If a cellular forensic tool successfully completes acquisition of the target device then all MMS messages and associated images shall be presented properly without modification. A_IM-19 If a cellular forensic tool successfully completes acquisition of the target device then all MMS messages and associated video shall be presented properly without modification.
Tester Name:	rpa
Test Host:	Morrisy
Test Date:	Thu Apr 3 10:15:44 EDT 2008
Device:	Nokia_6101
Source Setup:	OS: WIN XP Interface: cable

DATA OBJECTS	DATA ELEMENTS
Address Book Entries	
	Maximum Length
	Regular Length, email, picture
	Special Character
	Blank Name
	Regular Length, Deleted email - deleted picture
	Deleted Entry
	Foreign Entry
PIM Data	
	Maximum Length
	Regular Length
	Deleted Entry
	Special Character
Call Logs	
	Missed
	Missed - Deleted
	Incoming
	Incoming - Deleted
	Outgoing
	Outgoing - Deleted
Text Messages	
	Incoming SMS - Read
	Incoming SMS - Unread
	Incoming SMS - Deleted
	Outgoing SMS
	Outgoing SMS - Deleted
	Incoming EMS - Read
	Incoming EMS - Unread
	Incoming Foreign EMS - Read
	Incoming EMS - Deleted
	Outgoing EMS
	Outgoing EMS - Deleted
MMS Messages	
	Incoming Audio
	Incoming Image
	Incoming Video
	Outgoing Audio

		Outgoing Image
		Outgoing Video
	Stand-alone data files	
		Audio
		Audio - Deleted
		Image
		Image - Deleted
		Video
		Video - Deleted

Log Highlights:	Created By .XRY Version 3.6 Acquisition started: Thu Apr 3 10:15:44 EDT 2008 Acquisition finished: Thu Apr 3 10:39:34 EDT 2008 Device connectivity was established via supported interface Readability and completeness of acquired data was successful ALL MMS messages (Audio, Image, Video) were acquired **Notes:** QuickTime Version 7.4.1 was used to execute MMS attachments.

Results:	

Assertion & Expected Result	Actual Result
A IM-01 Device connectivity via supported interfaces.	as expected
A_IM-04 Readability and completeness of acquired data via supported reports.	as expected
A IM-17 Acquisition of audio MMS messages.	as expected
A IM-18 Acquisition of image MMS messages.	as expected
A IM-19 Acquisition of video MMS messages.	as expected

Analysis:	Expected results achieved

5.2.10   CFT-IM-10 (Nokia 6101)

Test Case CFT-IM-10 Micro Systemation .XRY Version 3.6	
Case Summary:	CFT-IM-10 Acquire mobile device internal memory and review reported stand-alone multi-media data (i.e., audio, graphics, video).
Assertions:	A_IM-01 If a cellular forensic tool provides support for connectivity of the target device then the tool shall successfully recognize the target device via all vendor supported interfaces (e.g., cable, Bluetooth, IrDA). A_IM-04 If a cellular forensic tool successfully completes acquisition of the target device then the tool shall have the ability to present acquired data elements in a human-readable format via either a preview-pane or generated report. A_IM-20 If a cellular forensic tool successfully completes acquisition of the target device then all stand-alone audio files shall be playable via either an internal application or suggested third-party application without modification. A_IM-21 If a cellular forensic tool successfully completes acquisition of the target device then all stand-alone image files shall be viewable via either an internal application or suggested third-party application without modification. A_IM-22 If a cellular forensic tool successfully completes acquisition of the target device then all stand-alone video files shall be viewable via either an internal application or suggested third-party application without modification.
Tester Name:	rpa
Test Host:	Morrisy
Test Date:	Thu Apr 3 11:56:48 EDT 2008
Device:	Nokia 6101
Source Setup:	OS: WIN XP Interface: cable

DATA OBJECTS	DATA ELEMENTS
Address Book Entries	
	Maximum Length
	Regular Length, email, picture
	Special Character
	Blank Name
	Regular Length, Deleted email - deleted picture
	Deleted Entry
	Foreign Entry
PIM Data	
	Maximum Length
	Regular Length
	Deleted Entry
	Special Character
Call Logs	
	Missed
	Missed - Deleted
	Incoming
	Incoming - Deleted
	Outgoing
	Outgoing - Deleted
Text Messages	
	Incoming SMS - Read
	Incoming SMS - Unread
	Incoming SMS - Deleted
	Outgoing SMS
	Outgoing SMS - Deleted
	Incoming EMS - Read
	Incoming EMS - Unread
	Incoming Foreign EMS - Read
	Incoming EMS - Deleted
	Outgoing EMS
	Outgoing EMS - Deleted
MMS Messages	
	Incoming Audio

		Incoming Image
		Incoming Video
		Outgoing Audio
		Outgoing Image
		Outgoing Video
Stand-alone data files		
		Audio
		Audio - Deleted
		Image
		Image - Deleted
		Video
		Video - Deleted

Log Highlights:	Created By .XRY Version 3.6 Acquisition started: Thu Apr 3 11:56:48 EDT 2008 Acquisition finished: Thu Apr 3 12:09:33 EDT 2008 Device connectivity was established via supported interface Readability and completeness of acquired data was successful ALL stand-alone data files (Audio, Image, Video) were acquired **Notes:** QuickTime Version 7.4.1 was used to execute stand-alone files.

Results:		

Assertion & Expected Result	Actual Result
A_IM-01 Device connectivity via supported interfaces.	as expected
A_IM-04 Readability and completeness of acquired data via supported reports.	as expected
A_IM-20 Acquisition of stand-alone audio files.	as expected
A_IM-21 Acquisition of stand-alone graphic files.	as expected
A_IM-22 Acquisition of stand-alone video files.	as expected

Analysis:	Expected results achieved

5.2.11   CFT-IMO-01   (Nokia 6101)

Test Case CFT-IMO-01 Micro Systemation .XRY Version 3.6	
Case Summary:	CFT-IMO-01 Acquire mobile device internal memory and review reported data via supported generated report formats.
Assertions:	A_IMO-38 If a cellular forensic tool successfully completes acquisition of the target device then the tool shall present the acquired data without modification via supported generated report formats.
Tester Name:	rpa
Test Host:	Morrisy
Test Date:	Fri Apr 11 08:40:04 EDT 2008
Device:	Nokia 6101
Source Setup:	OS: WIN XP Interface: cable

DATA OBJECTS	DATA ELEMENTS
Address Book Entries	
	Maximum Length
	Regular Length, email, picture
	Special Character
	Blank Name
	Regular Length, Deleted email - deleted picture
	Deleted Entry
	Foreign Entry
PIM Data	
	Maximum Length
	Regular Length
	Deleted Entry
	Special Character
Call Logs	
	Missed
	Missed - Deleted
	Incoming
	Incoming - Deleted
	Outgoing
	Outgoing - Deleted
Text Messages	
	Incoming SMS - Read
	Incoming SMS - Unread
	Incoming SMS - Deleted
	Outgoing SMS
	Outgoing SMS - Deleted
	Incoming EMS - Read
	Incoming EMS - Unread
	Incoming Foreign EMS - Read
	Incoming EMS - Deleted
	Outgoing EMS
	Outgoing EMS - Deleted
MMS Messages	
	Incoming Audio
	Incoming Image
	Incoming Video
	Outgoing Audio
	Outgoing Image
	Outgoing Video
Stand-alone data files	
	Audio
	Audio - Deleted
	Image
	Image - Deleted
	Video
	Video - Deleted

Log	Created By .XRY Version 3.6

Test Case CFT-IMO-01 Micro Systemation .XRY Version 3.6		
Highlights:	Acquisition started: Fri Apr 11 08:40:04 EDT 2008 Acquisition finished: Fri Apr 11 09:06:33 EDT 2008 Complete representation of known data via generated reports was successful	
Results:		

Assertion & Expected Result	Actual Result
A_IMO-38 Comparison of known device data elements via generated reports.	as expected

Analysis:	Expected results achieved

5.2.12   CFT-IMO-02   (Nokia 6101)

Test Case CFT-IMO-02 Micro Systemation .XRY Version 3.6	
Case Summary:	CFT-IMO-02 Acquire mobile device internal memory and review reported data via the preview-pane.
Assertions:	A_IMO-39 If a cellular forensic tool successfully completes acquisition of the target device then the tool shall present the acquired data without modification in a preview-pane view.
Tester Name:	rpa
Test Host:	Morrisy
Test Date:	Fri Apr 11 09:12:33 EDT 2008
Device:	Nokia 6101
Source Setup:	OS: WIN XP Interface: cable

DATA OBJECTS	DATA ELEMENTS
Address Book Entries	
	Maximum Length
	Regular Length, email, picture
	Special Character
	Blank Name
	Regular Length, Deleted email - deleted picture
	Deleted Entry
	Foreign Entry
PIM Data	
	Maximum Length
	Regular Length
	Deleted Entry
	Special Character
Call Logs	
	Missed
	Missed - Deleted
	Incoming
	Incoming - Deleted
	Outgoing
	Outgoing - Deleted
Text Messages	
	Incoming SMS - Read
	Incoming SMS - Unread
	Incoming SMS - Deleted
	Outgoing SMS
	Outgoing SMS - Deleted
	Incoming EMS - Read
	Incoming EMS - Unread
	Incoming Foreign EMS - Read
	Incoming EMS - Deleted
	Outgoing EMS
	Outgoing EMS - Deleted
MMS Messages	
	Incoming Audio
	Incoming Image
	Incoming Video
	Outgoing Audio
	Outgoing Image
	Outgoing Video
Stand-alone data files	
	Audio
	Audio - Deleted
	Image
	Image - Deleted
	Video
	Video - Deleted

Log	Created By .XRY Version 3.6

Test Case CFT-IMO-02 Micro Systemation .XRY Version 3.6	
Highlights:	Acquisition started: Fri Apr 11 09:12:33 EDT 2008 Acquisition finished: Fri Apr 11 09:25:20 EDT 2008 Complete representation of known data via preview-pane was successful
Results:	

Assertion & Expected Result	Actual Result
A_IMO-39 Comparison of known device data elements via preview-pane.	as expected

Analysis:	Expected results achieved

5.2.13   CFT-IMO-03   (Nokia 6101)

Test Case CFT-IMO-03 Micro Systemation .XRY Version 3.6	
Case Summary:	CFT-IMO-03 Acquire mobile device internal memory and compare reported data via the preview-pane and supported generated reports.
Assertions:	A_IMO-38 If a cellular forensic tool successfully completes acquisition of the target device then the tool shall present the acquired data without modification via supported generated report formats. A_IMO-39 If a cellular forensic tool successfully completes acquisition of the target device then the tool shall present the acquired data without modification in a preview-pane view. A_IMO-40 If a cellular forensic tool provides a preview-pane view and a generated report of the acquired data then the reports shall maintain consistency of all reported data elements.
Tester Name:	rpa
Test Host:	Morrisy
Test Date:	Fri Apr 11 09:26:40 EDT 2008
Device:	Nokia 6101
Source Setup:	OS: WIN XP Interface: cable

DATA OBJECTS	DATA ELEMENTS
Address Book Entries	
	Maximum Length
	Regular Length, email, picture
	Special Character
	Blank Name
	Regular Length, Deleted email - deleted picture
	Deleted Entry
	Foreign Entry
PIM Data	
	Maximum Length
	Regular Length
	Deleted Entry
	Special Character
Call Logs	
	Missed
	Missed - Deleted
	Incoming
	Incoming - Deleted
	Outgoing
	Outgoing - Deleted
Text Messages	
	Incoming SMS - Read
	Incoming SMS - Unread
	Incoming SMS - Deleted
	Outgoing SMS
	Outgoing SMS - Deleted
	Incoming EMS - Read
	Incoming EMS - Unread
	Incoming Foreign EMS - Read
	Incoming EMS - Deleted
	Outgoing EMS
	Outgoing EMS - Deleted
MMS Messages	
	Incoming Audio
	Incoming Image
	Incoming Video
	Outgoing Audio
	Outgoing Image
	Outgoing Video
Stand-alone data files	
	Audio
	Audio - Deleted
	Image
	Image - Deleted
	Video

Test Case CFT-IMO-03 Micro Systemation .XRY Version 3.6	
	Video - Deleted
Log Highlights:	Created By .XRY Version 3.6 Acquisition started: Fri Apr 11 09:26:40 EDT 2008 Acquisition finished: Fri Apr 11 09:40:51 EDT 2008 Complete representation of known data via generated reports was successful Complete representation of known data via preview-pane was successful Consistency between generated reports and preview-pane was successful

Results:

Assertion & Expected Result	Actual Result
A_IMO-38 Comparison of known device data elements via generated reports.	as expected
A_IMO-39 Comparison of known device data elements via preview-pane.	as expected
A_IMO-40 Compare generated reports and preview-pane views for device acquisition.	as expected

Analysis:	Expected results achieved

5.2.14   CFT-IMO-04   (Nokia 6101)

Test Case CFT-IMO-04 Micro Systemation .XRY Version 3.6	
Case Summary:	CFT-IMO-04 After a successful mobile device internal memory acquisition, alter the case file via third party means and attempt to re-open the case.
Assertions:	A_IMO-41 If modification is attempted to the case file or individual data elements via third-party means then the tool shall provide protection mechanisms disallowing or reporting data modification.
Tester Name:	rpa
Test Host:	Morrisy
Test Date:	Fri Apr 11 09:42:14 EDT 2008
Device:	Nokia 6101
Source Setup:	OS: WIN XP Interface: cable

DATA OBJECTS	DATA ELEMENTS
Address Book Entries	
	Maximum Length
	Regular Length, email, picture
	Special Character
	Blank Name
	Regular Length, Deleted email - deleted picture
	Deleted Entry
	Foreign Entry
PIM Data	
	Maximum Length
	Regular Length
	Deleted Entry
	Special Character
Call Logs	
	Missed
	Missed - Deleted
	Incoming
	Incoming - Deleted
	Outgoing
	Outgoing - Deleted
Text Messages	
	Incoming SMS - Read
	Incoming SMS - Unread
	Incoming SMS - Deleted
	Outgoing SMS
	Outgoing SMS - Deleted
	Incoming EMS - Read
	Incoming EMS - Unread
	Incoming Foreign EMS - Read
	Incoming EMS - Deleted
	Outgoing EMS
	Outgoing EMS - Deleted
MMS Messages	
	Incoming Audio
	Incoming Image
	Incoming Video
	Outgoing Audio
	Outgoing Image
	Outgoing Video
Stand-alone data files	
	Audio
	Audio - Deleted
	Image
	Image - Deleted
	Video
	Video - Deleted

Log	Created By .XRY Version 3.6

Test Case CFT-IMO-04 Micro Systemation .XRY Version 3.6	
Highlights:	Acquisition started: Fri Apr 11 09:42:14 EDT 2008 Acquisition finished: Fri Apr 11 10:05:25 EDT 2008 Notification of modified case data was successful **Notes**: Case File Encryption has to be selected before acquisition.
Results:	

Assertion & Expected Result	Actual Result
A_IMO-41 Notification of modified device case data.	as expected

Analysis:	Expected results achieved

5.2.15 CFT-IMO-07 (Nokia 6101)

Test Case CFT-IMO-07 Micro Systemation .XRY Version 3.6	
Case Summary:	CFT-IMO-07 Create a SIM access card via vendor documentation.
Assertions:	A_IMO-51 If the cellular forensic tool supports SIM access card creation then the card creation shall be completed without errors via manufacturer suggested protocols. Access cards characteristics should be consistent with vendor documentation.
Tester Name:	rpa
Test Host:	Morrisy
Test Date:	Fri Apr 11 11:00:15 EDT 2008
Device:	TMOBILE SIM
Source Setup:	OS: WIN XP Interface: USB

DATA OBJECTS	DATA ELEMENTS
Address Book Entries	
	Maximum Length
	Regular Length, email, picture
	Special Character
	Blank Name
	Regular Length, Deleted email - deleted picture
	Deleted Entry
	Foreign Entry
PIM Data	
	Maximum Length
	Regular Length
	Deleted Entry
	Special Character
Call Logs	
	Missed
	Missed - Deleted
	Incoming
	Incoming - Deleted
	Outgoing
	Outgoing - Deleted
Text Messages	
	Incoming SMS - Read
	Incoming SMS - Unread
	Incoming SMS - Deleted
	Outgoing SMS
	Outgoing SMS - Deleted
	Incoming EMS - Read
	Incoming EMS - Unread
	Incoming Foreign EMS - Read
	Incoming EMS - Deleted
	Outgoing EMS
	Outgoing EMS - Deleted
MMS Messages	
	Incoming Audio
	Incoming Image
	Incoming Video
	Outgoing Audio
	Outgoing Image
	Outgoing Video
Stand-alone data files	
	Audio
	Audio - Deleted
	Image
	Image - Deleted
	Video
	Video - Deleted

Test Case CFT-IMO-07 Micro Systemation .XRY Version 3.6	
Log Highlights:	Created By .XRY Version 3.6 Acquisition started: Fri Apr 11 11:00:15 EDT 2008 Acquisition finished: Fri Apr 11 11:02:23 EDT 2008 Access card creation was successful
Results:	

Assertion & Expected Result	Actual Result
A IMO-51 Access card creation.	as expected

Analysis:	Expected results achieved

5.2.16   CFT-IMO-08   (Nokia 6101)

Test Case CFT-IMO-08 Micro Systemation .XRY Version 3.6	
Case Summary:	CFT-IMO-08 Acquire mobile device internal memory and review generated log files.
Assertions:	A_IMO-52 If the cellular forensic tool supports log creation then the application should present the log files outlining the acquisition process in a human-readable format.
Tester Name:	rpa
Test Host:	Morrisy
Test Date:	Fri Apr 11 11:04:15 EDT 2008
Device:	Nokia 6101
Source Setup:	OS: WIN XP Interface: cable

DATA OBJECTS	DATA ELEMENTS
Address Book Entries	
	Maximum Length
	Regular Length, email, picture
	Special Character
	Blank Name
	Regular Length, Deleted email - deleted picture
	Deleted Entry
	Foreign Entry
PIM Data	
	Maximum Length
	Regular Length
	Deleted Entry
	Special Character
Call Logs	
	Missed
	Missed - Deleted
	Incoming
	Incoming - Deleted
	Outgoing
	Outgoing - Deleted
Text Messages	
	Incoming SMS - Read
	Incoming SMS - Unread
	Incoming SMS - Deleted
	Outgoing SMS
	Outgoing SMS - Deleted
	Incoming EMS - Read
	Incoming EMS - Unread
	Incoming Foreign EMS - Read
	Incoming EMS - Deleted
	Outgoing EMS
	Outgoing EMS - Deleted
MMS Messages	
	Incoming Audio
	Incoming Image
	Incoming Video
	Outgoing Audio
	Outgoing Image
	Outgoing Video
Stand-alone data files	
	Audio
	Audio - Deleted
	Image
	Image - Deleted
	Video
	Video - Deleted

```
Test Case CFT-IMO-08 Micro Systemation .XRY Version 3.6
```

Log	Created By .XRY Version 3.6
Highlights:	Acquisition started: Fri Apr 11 11:04:15 EDT 2008
	Acquisition finished: Fri Apr 11 11:25:12 EDT 2008

```
          Creation of complete and human-readable log files was successful


          Notes:
          XRY Log

          Module  Status      Message
          ------  -------     -------
          MAIN    Success     Initiating Process
          MAIN    Success     .XRY Version 3.6
          MAIN    Success     Connected to SoftGSM NG USB Modem #5 [COM9]
          MAIN    Success     Device Name: Nokia 6101
          MAIN    Success     CGMI Resp = [Nokia]
          MAIN    Success     CGMM Resp = [Nokia 6101]
          MAIN    Success     CGMR Resp = [V 03.3508-06-05RM-76(c) Nokia.  ]
          MAIN    Success     I3 Resp = [Nokia 6101]
          MAIN    Success     Starting process of GSM0707 (3.1)
          GSM0707 Success     Connecting
          GSM0707 Success     Analyzing General Information
          GSM0707 Success     Reading General Information
          GSM0707 Success     Disconnecting
          MAIN    Success     GSM0707 (3.1) completed successfully
          MAIN    Success     Starting process of FBUS (3.1)
          FBUS    Success     Connecting
          FBUS    Success     Analyzing
          FBUS    Success     Reading General Information
          FBUS    Success     Analyzing Contacts ME
          FBUS    Success     Reading Contacts
          FBUS    Success     Analyzing Contacts SM
          FBUS    Success     Reading Contacts
          FBUS    Success     Analyzing Calls
          FBUS    Success     Reading Calls
          FBUS    Success     Reading Calls
          FBUS    Success     Reading Calls
          FBUS    Success     Analyzing Calendar
          FBUS    Success     Reading Calendar
          FBUS    Success     Analyzing SMS
          FBUS    Success     Reading SMS
          FBUS    Success     Reading Inbox
          FBUS    Success     Reading Sent items
          FBUS    Success     Reading Saved text msgs.
          FBUS    Success     Reading Templates
          FBUS    Success     Reading Outbox
          FBUS    Success     Reading Outbox
          FBUS    Success     Analyzing Tasks
          FBUS    Success     Analyzing Notes
          FBUS    Success     Reading Notes
          FBUS    Success     Analyzing Files
          FBUS    Success     Analyzing predefgallery
          FBUS    Success     Analyzing predefgallery/predeftones
          FBUS    Success     Analyzing predefgallery/predeftones/predefringtones
          FBUS    Success     Analyzing predefgallery/predeftones/predefalerttones
          FBUS    Success     Analyzing predefgallery/predefgraphics
          FBUS    Success     Analyzing
          predefgallery/predefgraphics/predefwallpapers
          FBUS    Success     Analyzing
          predefgallery/predefgraphics/predefscreensavers
          FBUS    Success     Analyzing predefgallery/predefgraphics/predefcliparts
          FBUS    Success     Analyzing predefgallery/predefgraphics/predefframes
          FBUS    Success     Analyzing
          predefgallery/predefgraphics/predefpresencelogo
          FBUS    Success     Analyzing predefgallery/predefthemes
          FBUS    Success     Analyzing predefgallery/predefthemeactive
          FBUS    Success     Analyzing
          predefgallery/predefthemeactive/themes_setup1
          FBUS    Success     Analyzing predefgallery/predefphotos
          FBUS    Success     Analyzing predefgallery/predefvideos
```

FBUS	Success	Analyzing predefgallery/predefrecordings
FBUS	Success	Analyzing predefgallery/predefreceived
FBUS	Success	Analyzing predefgallery/predefthemepreview
FBUS	Success	Analyzing predefgallery/predefthemepreview/Thumbnails
FBUS	Success	Analyzing predefinfofolder
FBUS	Success	Analyzing predefomadm
FBUS	Success	Analyzing predefomadm/PRECFG
FBUS	Success	Analyzing predefomadm/01
FBUS	Success	Analyzing predefomadm/01/19
FBUS	Success	Analyzing predefomadm/01/01
FBUS	Success	Analyzing predefomadm/01/02
FBUS	Success	Analyzing predefomadm/01/03
FBUS	Success	Analyzing predefomadm/01/04
FBUS	Success	Analyzing predefomadm/02
FBUS	Success	Analyzing predefomadm/02/19
FBUS	Success	Analyzing predefomadm/02/01
FBUS	Success	Analyzing predefomadm/02/02
FBUS	Success	Analyzing predefomadm/02/03
FBUS	Success	Analyzing predefomadm/02/04
FBUS	Success	Analyzing predefjava
FBUS	Success	Analyzing predefjava/predefcollections
FBUS	Success	Analyzing predefjava/predefgames
FBUS	Success	Analyzing predefhiddenfolder
FBUS	Success	Analyzing predefhiddenfolder/predefWVPreload
FBUS	Success	Analyzing predefhiddenfolder/predefdrmrights
FBUS	Success	Analyzing predefhiddenfolder/predefpbimgs
FBUS	Success	Analyzing predefhiddenfolder/predefvoicemodels
FBUS	Success	Analyzing predefhiddenfolder/predefvoiceprompts
FBUS	Success	Analyzing predefhiddenfolder/predefwvlogos
FBUS	Success	Analyzing predefhiddenfolder/predefmenus
FBUS	Success	Analyzing predefmenuapps
FBUS	Success	Analyzing predefmenuapps/predefemail
FBUS	Success	Analyzing predefmenuapps/predefsms
FBUS	Success	Analyzing predefmenuapps/predefimclient
FBUS	Success	Analyzing predefmessages
FBUS	Success	Analyzing predefmessages/predefinbox
FBUS	Success	Analyzing predefmessages/predefoutbox
FBUS	Success	Analyzing predefmessages/predefsent
FBUS	Success	Analyzing predefmessages/predefdrafts
FBUS	Success	Analyzing predeftemp
FBUS	Success	Analyzing predeffiledownload
FBUS	Success	Analyzing HTTP
FBUS	Success	Analyzing HTTP/opmenu
FBUS	Success	Analyzing HTTP/cookie
FBUS	Success	Analyzing HTTP/cache
FBUS	Success	Analyzing predefsyncml
FBUS	Success	Analyzing predefcalendar
FBUS	Success	Analyzing serviceapplication
FBUS	Success	Reading User Content Package r
FBUS	Success	Reading FIM_perm_id
FBUS	Success	Reading FIM_fixed_id
FBUS	Success	Reading Acrobatics.mid
FBUS	Success	Reading Caribbean.mid
FBUS	Success	Reading Cycle.mid
FBUS	Success	Reading Espionage.mid
FBUS	Success	Reading Farewell.mid
FBUS	Success	Reading Jig.mid
FBUS	Success	Reading Low.mid
FBUS	Success	Reading Nokia tune.mid
FBUS	Success	Reading Nocturnal.mid
FBUS	Success	Reading Repose.mid
FBUS	Success	Reading River cruise.mid
FBUS	Success	Reading Swept away.mid
FBUS	Success	Reading Robotique.mp3
FBUS	Success	Reading Playing_tricks.mp3
FBUS	Success	Reading Fete.mp3
FBUS	Success	Reading Cackle.mp3
FBUS	Success	Reading Graffiti.mp3
FBUS	Success	Reading Message 1.mid
FBUS	Success	Reading Message 2.mid

FBUS	Success	Reading Message 3.mid
FBUS	Success	Reading Message 4.mid
FBUS	Success	Reading Splash.jpg
FBUS	Success	Reading Flower.jpg
FBUS	Success	Reading Marbles.jpg
FBUS	Success	Reading Mountains.jpg
FBUS	Success	Reading Pink.jpg
FBUS	Success	Reading Colors.jpg
FBUS	Success	Reading Golden Years.jpg
FBUS	Success	Reading Goldfish.jpg
FBUS	Success	Reading Vintage.jpg
FBUS	Success	Reading Cells.gif
FBUS	Success	Reading Neon.gif
FBUS	Success	Reading Clip-art05.gif
FBUS	Success	Reading Clip-art06.gif
FBUS	Success	Reading Clip-art01.gif
FBUS	Success	Reading Clip-art02.gif
FBUS	Success	Reading Clip-art03.gif
FBUS	Success	Reading Clip-art04.gif
FBUS	Success	Reading Clip-art07.gif
FBUS	Success	Reading Clip-art08.gif
FBUS	Success	Reading Clip-art09.gif
FBUS	Success	Reading Clip-art10.gif
FBUS	Success	Reading Frame01.gif
FBUS	Success	Reading Frame02.gif
FBUS	Success	Reading Frame03.gif
FBUS	Success	Reading Frame04.gif
FBUS	Success	Reading Frame05.gif
FBUS	Success	Reading Frame06.gif
FBUS	Success	Reading Frame07.gif
FBUS	Success	Reading Frame08.gif
FBUS	Success	Reading Frame09.gif
FBUS	Success	Reading Frame10.gif
FBUS	Success	Reading Pres_01.gif
FBUS	Success	Reading Pres_02.gif
FBUS	Success	Reading Pres_04.gif
FBUS	Success	Reading Pres_03.gif
FBUS	Success	Reading Pres_05.gif
FBUS	Success	Reading Pres_06.gif
FBUS	Success	Reading Pres_07.gif
FBUS	Success	Reading Pres_08.gif
FBUS	Success	Reading Pres_09.gif
FBUS	Success	Reading Pres_10.gif
FBUS	Success	Reading Window.nth
FBUS	Success	Reading Circle.nth
FBUS	Success	Reading Basic.nth
FBUS	Success	Reading themes.ini
FBUS	Success	Reading theme_descriptor.xml
FBUS	Success	Reading Window_ss.gif
FBUS	Success	Reading Window_wp.jpg
FBUS	Success	Reading Window_wp_mini.jpg
FBUS	Success	Reading Nokia_tune.mid
FBUS	Success	Reading large_thumbnail.gif
FBUS	Success	Reading small_thumbnail.gif
FBUS	Success	Reading Window_bk_mini.png
FBUS	Success	Reading Window_bk.png
FBUS	Success	Reading Sunset.jpg
FBUS	Success	Reading emma.jpg
FBUS	Success	Reading Video000.3gp
FBUS	Success	Reading Video001.3gp
FBUS	Success	Reading chare.wav
FBUS	Success	Reading french.mp3
FBUS	Success	Reading SuiteConf.xml
FBUS	Success	Reading bootstrap_app_no_network
FBUS	Success	Reading USER_DATA
FBUS	Success	Reading HLOG
FBUS	Success	Reading 01
FBUS	Success	Reading 01
FBUS	Success	Reading 01
FBUS	Success	Reading 01

FBUS	Success	Reading 01
FBUS	Success	Reading HLOG
FBUS	Success	Reading 01
FBUS	Success	Reading 01
FBUS	Success	Reading 01
FBUS	Success	Reading 01
FBUS	Success	Reading 01
FBUS	Success	Reading kqq_en_zh-CN_zh-TW.jad
FBUS	Success	Reading kqq_en_zh-CN_zh-TW.jar
FBUS	Success	Reading soli_en_zh-CN_zh-TW.jad
FBUS	Success	Reading soli_en_zh-CN_zh-TW.jar
FBUS	Success	Reading gtour_en_zh-CN_zh-TW.jad
FBUS	Success	Reading gtour_en_zh-CN_zh-TW.jar
FBUS	Success	Reading pipe_en_zh-CN_zh-TW.jad
FBUS	Success	Reading pipe_en_zh-CN_zh-TW.jar
FBUS	Success	Reading _jmr_suite_list_file.jmr
FBUS	Success	Reading _jmr_suite_attrib_file.jmr
FBUS	Success	Reading _jmr_suite_contents_file.jmr
FBUS	Success	Reading jps_connection_registry_file.reg
FBUS	Success	Reading jps_timer_registry_file.reg
FBUS	Success	Reading UPF_General_data
FBUS	Success	Reading UPF_Silent_data
FBUS	Success	Reading UPF_Meeting_data
FBUS	Success	Reading UPF_Outdoor_data
FBUS	Success	Reading UPF_Mystyle1_data
FBUS	Success	Reading UPF_Mystyle2_data
FBUS	Success	Reading wv1.gif
FBUS	Success	Reading wv2.gif
FBUS	Success	Reading wv3.gif
FBUS	Success	Reading wv4.gif
FBUS	Success	Reading PBImg.jpeg
FBUS	Success	Reading PBImg000.jpeg
FBUS	Success	Reading emcl3_en_zh-CN_zh-TW.jad
FBUS	Success	Reading emcl3_en_zh-CN_zh-TW.jar
FBUS	Success	Reading 6 34631B47250 22+12404213651 ˙ TYPE=PLMN1
FBUS	Success	Reading C 34631DE1250 22+12404213651 ˙ TYPE=PLMN1
FBUS	Success	Reading 9 34631C7A250 22+12404213651 ˙ TYPE=PLMN1
FBUS	Success	Reading 1 34630EE6210 202404470381 ˙ TYPE=PLMN1
FBUS	Success	Reading 2 3463109B210 202404470381 ˙ TYPE=PLMN1
FBUS	Success	Reading 3 346315A2210 202404470381 ˙ TYPE=PLMN1
FBUS	Success	Reading CYRL2WfUgTu4D7Ocy.hdr
FBUS	Success	Reading CYRL2WfUgTu4D7Ocy.dat
FBUS	Success	Reading C2LZoveTPg9GqyzDF.hdr
FBUS	Success	Reading C2LZoveTPg9GqyzDF.dat
FBUS	Success	Disconnecting
MAIN	Success	FBUS (3.1) completed successfully
MAIN	Success	Processing completed successfully.
MAIN	Success	Total processing time: 10 minutes, 11 seconds
MAIN	Success	13 items read to General Information folder
MAIN	Success	17 items read to Contacts folder
MAIN	Success	5 items read to Calendar folder
MAIN	Success	2 items read to Notes folder
MAIN	Success	36 items read to SMS folder
MAIN	Success	6 items read to MMS folder
MAIN	Success	56 items read to Pictures folder
MAIN	Success	2 items read to Videos folder
MAIN	Success	24 items read to Audio folder
MAIN	Success	48 items read to Files folder

Results:

Assertion & Expected Result	Actual Result
A_IMO-52 Device Log file output.	as expected

Analysis: Expected results achieved

5.2.17　　CFT-IMO-09　　(Nokia 6101)

Test Case CFT-IMO-09 Micro Systemation .XRY Version 3.6	
Case Summary:	CFT-IMO-09 Acquire mobile device internal memory and review data containing foreign language characters.
Assertions:	A_IMO-38 If a cellular forensic tool successfully completes acquisition of the target device then the tool shall present the acquired data without modification via supported generated report formats. A_IMO-39 If a cellular forensic tool successfully completes acquisition of the target device then the tool shall present the acquired data without modification in a preview-pane view. A_IMO-53 If the cellular forensic tool supports proper display of foreign language character sets then the application should present address book entries containing foreign language characters in their native format without modification. A_IMO-54 If the cellular forensic tool supports proper display of foreign language character sets then the application should present text messages containing foreign language characters in their native format without modification.
Tester Name:	rpa
Test Host:	Morrisy
Test Date:	Fri Apr 11 11:26:14 EDT 2008
Device:	Nokia 6101
Source Setup:	OS: WIN XP Interface: cable

DATA OBJECTS	DATA ELEMENTS
Address Book Entries	
	Maximum Length
	Regular Length, email, picture
	Special Character
	Blank Name
	Regular Length, Deleted email - deleted picture
	Deleted Entry
	Foreign Entry
PIM Data	
	Maximum Length
	Regular Length
	Deleted Entry
	Special Character
Call Logs	
	Missed
	Missed - Deleted
	Incoming
	Incoming - Deleted
	Outgoing
	Outgoing - Deleted
Text Messages	
	Incoming SMS - Read
	Incoming SMS - Unread
	Incoming SMS - Deleted
	Outgoing SMS
	Outgoing SMS - Deleted
	Incoming EMS - Read
	Incoming EMS - Unread
	Incoming Foreign EMS - Read
	Incoming EMS - Deleted
	Outgoing EMS
	Outgoing EMS - Deleted
MMS Messages	
	Incoming Audio
	Incoming Image
	Incoming Video
	Outgoing Audio
	Outgoing Image
	Outgoing Video

Test Case CFT-IMO-09 Micro Systemation .XRY Version 3.6

	Stand-alone data files	
		Audio
		Audio - Deleted
		Image
		Image - Deleted
		Video
		Video - Deleted

Log Highlights:	Created By .XRY Version 3.6 Acquisition started: Fri Apr 11 11:26:14 EDT 2008 Acquisition finished: Fri Apr 11 11:35:11 EDT 2008 Complete representation of known data via generated reports was successful Complete representation of known data via preview-pane was successful Foreign character Address book entries were acquired and properly displayed Foreign character text messages were acquired and properly displayed

Results:		
	Assertion & Expected Result	**Actual Result**
	A_IMO-38 Comparison of known device data elements via generated reports.	as expected
	A_IMO-39 Comparison of known device data elements via preview-pane.	as expected
	A_IMO-53 Acquisition of address book entries containing foreign language characters.	as expected
	A_IMO-54 Acquisition of outgoing text messages containing foreign language characters.	as expected

Analysis:	Expected results achieved

5.2.18   CFT-IMO-11   (Nokia 6101)

Test Case CFT-IMO-11 Micro Systemation .XRY Version 3.6	
Case Summary:	CFT-IMO-11 Acquire mobile device internal memory and review hash values for vendor supported data objects.
Assertions:	A_IMO-38 If a cellular forensic tool successfully completes acquisition of the target device then the tool shall present the acquired data without modification via supported generated report formats. A_IMO-39 If a cellular forensic tool successfully completes acquisition of the target device then the tool shall present the acquired data without modification in a preview-pane view. A_IMO-56 If the cellular forensic tool supports hashing for individual data objects then the tool shall present the user with a hash value for each supported data object.
Tester Name:	rpa
Test Host:	Morrisy
Test Date:	Fri Apr 11 11:48:13 EDT 2008
Device:	Nokia 6101
Source Setup:	OS: WIN XP Interface: cable

DATA OBJECTS	DATA ELEMENTS
Address Book Entries	
	Maximum Length
	Regular Length, email, picture
	Special Character
	Blank Name
	Regular Length, Deleted email - deleted picture
	Deleted Entry
	Foreign Entry
PIM Data	
	Maximum Length
	Regular Length
	Deleted Entry
	Special Character
Call Logs	
	Missed
	Missed - Deleted
	Incoming
	Incoming - Deleted
	Outgoing
	Outgoing - Deleted
Text Messages	
	Incoming SMS - Read
	Incoming SMS - Unread
	Incoming SMS - Deleted
	Outgoing SMS
	Outgoing SMS - Deleted
	Incoming EMS - Read
	Incoming EMS - Unread
	Incoming Foreign EMS - Read
	Incoming EMS - Deleted
	Outgoing EMS
	Outgoing EMS - Deleted
MMS Messages	
	Incoming Audio
	Incoming Image
	Incoming Video
	Outgoing Audio
	Outgoing Image
	Outgoing Video
Stand-alone data files	
	Audio
	Audio - Deleted
	Image

	Image - Deleted
	Video
	Video - Deleted

Log Highlights:	Created By .XRY Version 3.6 Acquisition started: Fri Apr 11 11:48:13 EDT 2008 Acquisition finished: Fri Apr 11 12:01:34 EDT 2008 Complete representation of known data via generated reports was successful Complete representation of known data via preview-pane was successful Device hash reporting for individual acquired data elements was successful **Notes**: SHA1 and MD5 hashes were successfully calculated for pictures, video, audio and stand-alone files.

Results:		
	Assertion & Expected Result	**Actual Result**
	A_IMO-38 Comparison of known device data elements via generated reports.	as expected
	A_IMO-39 Comparison of known device data elements via preview-pane.	as expected
	A_IMO-56 Device hash reporting for individual acquired data objects.	as expected
Analysis:	Expected results achieved	

5.2.19   CFT-SIM-01   (T-Mobile SIM)

Test Case CFT-SIM-01 Micro Systemation .XRY Version 3.6	
Case Summary:	CFT-SIM-01 Acquire SIM over supported interfaces (e.g., PC/SC reader, proprietary reader).
Assertions:	A_SIM-23 If a cellular forensic tool provides support for connectivity of the target SIM then the tool shall successfully recognize the target SIM via all vendor supported interfaces (e.g., PC/SC reader, proprietary reader).
Tester Name:	rpa
Test Host:	Morrisy
Test Date:	Thu Apr 3 12:32:32 EDT 2008
Device:	TMOBILE SIM
Source Setup:	OS: WIN XP Interface: USB

DATA OBJECTS	DATA ELEMENTS
Abbreviated Dialing Numbers (ADN)	
	Maximum Length
	Special Character
	Blank Name
	Regular Length - Deleted Number
	Foreign Entry
Call Logs	
	Last Numbers Dialed (LND)
Text Messages	
	Incoming SMS - Read
	Incoming SMS - Foreign
	Incoming SMS - Deleted
	Incoming SMS - Unread
	Incoming Foreign EMS - Read
	Incoming EMS - Deleted

Log Highlights:	Created By .XRY Version 3.6 Acquisition started: Thu Apr 3 12:32:32 EDT 2008 Acquisition finished: Thu Apr 3 12:36:57 EDT 2008 Media connectivity was established via supported interface

Results:		

Assertion & Expected Result	Actual Result
A_SIM-23 SIM connectivity via supported interfaces.	as expected

Analysis:	Expected results achieved

5.2.20　CFT-SIM-02　(T-Mobile SIM)

Test Case CFT-SIM-02 Micro Systemation .XRY Version 3.6	
Case Summary:	CFT-SIM-02 Attempt acquisition of a non-supported SIM.
Assertions:	A_SIM-24 If a cellular forensic tool attempts to connect to a non-supported SIM then the tool shall have the ability to identify that the SIM is not supported.
Tester Name:	rpa
Test Host:	Morrisy
Test Date:	Thu Apr 3 12:38:38 EDT 2008
Device:	TMOBILE SIM
Source Setup:	OS: WIN XP Interface: USB

DATA OBJECTS	DATA ELEMENTS
Abbreviated Dialing Numbers (ADN)	
	Maximum Length
	Special Character
	Blank Name
	Regular Length - Deleted Number
	Foreign Entry
Call Logs	
	Last Numbers Dialed (LND)
Text Messages	
	Incoming SMS - Read
	Incoming SMS - Foreign
	Incoming SMS - Deleted
	Incoming SMS - Unread
	Incoming Foreign EMS - Read
	Incoming EMS - Deleted

Log Highlights:	Created By .XRY Version 3.6 Acquisition started: Thu Apr 3 12:38:38 EDT 2008 Acquisition finished: Thu Apr 3 12:40:04 EDT 2008 Identification of non-supported media was successful
Results:	

Assertion & Expected Result	Actual Result
A_SIM-24 Identification of non-supported SIMs.	as expected

Analysis:	Expected results achieved

5.2.21   CFT-SIM-03   (T-Mobile SIM)

Test Case CFT-SIM-03 Micro Systemation .XRY Version 3.6	
Case Summary:	CFT-SIM-03 Begin SIM acquisition and interrupt connectivity by interface disengagement.
Assertions:	A_SIM-23 If a cellular forensic tool provides support for connectivity of the target SIM then the tool shall successfully recognize the target SIM via all vendor supported interfaces (e.g., PC/SC reader, proprietary reader). A_SIM-25 If a cellular forensic tool encounters disengagement between the SIM reader and application then the application shall notify the user that connectivity has been disrupted.
Tester Name:	rpa
Test Host:	Morrisy
Test Date:	Thu Apr 3 12:41:18 EDT 2008
Device:	TMOBILE_SIM
Source Setup:	OS: WIN XP Interface: USB

DATA OBJECTS	DATA ELEMENTS
Abbreviated Dialing Numbers (ADN)	
	Maximum Length
	Special Character
	Blank Name
	Regular Length - Deleted Number
	Foreign Entry
Call Logs	
	Last Numbers Dialed (LND)
Text Messages	
	Incoming SMS - Read
	Incoming SMS - Foreign
	Incoming SMS - Deleted
	Incoming SMS - Unread
	Incoming Foreign EMS - Read
	Incoming EMS - Deleted

Log Highlights:	Created By .XRY Version 3.6 Acquisition started: Thu Apr 3 12:41:18 EDT 2008 Acquisition finished: Thu Apr 3 12:42:43 EDT 2008 Media connectivity was established via supported interface Media acquisition disruption notification was successful
Results:	

Assertion & Expected Result	Actual Result
A_SIM-23 SIM connectivity via supported interfaces.	as expected
A_SIM-25 Notification of SIM acquisition disruption.	as expected

Analysis:	Expected results achieved

5.2.22   CFT-SIM-04   (T-Mobile SIM)

Test Case CFT-SIM-04 Micro Systemation .XRY Version 3.6	
Case Summary:	CFT-SIM-04 Attempt acquisition on a password-protected SIM.
Assertions:	A_SIM-23 If a cellular forensic tool provides support for connectivity of the target SIM then the tool shall successfully recognize the target SIM via all vendor supported interfaces (e.g., PC/SC reader, proprietary reader). A_SIM-26 If the SIM is password-protected then the cellular forensic tool shall provide the examiner with the opportunity to input the PIN before acquisition.
Tester Name:	rpa
Test Host:	Morrisy
Test Date:	Thu Apr 3 12:44:22 EDT 2008
Device:	TMOBILE SIM
Source Setup:	OS: WIN XP Interface: USB

DATA OBJECTS	DATA ELEMENTS
Abbreviated Dialing Numbers (ADN)	
	Maximum Length
	Special Character
	Blank Name
	Regular Length - Deleted Number
	Foreign Entry
Call Logs	
	Last Numbers Dialed (LND)
Text Messages	
	Incoming SMS - Read
	Incoming SMS - Foreign
	Incoming SMS - Deleted
	Incoming SMS - Unread
	Incoming Foreign EMS - Read
	Incoming EMS - Deleted

Log Highlights:	Created By .XRY Version 3.6 Acquisition started: Thu Apr 3 12:44:22 EDT 2008 Acquisition finished: Thu Apr 3 12:45:47 EDT 2008 Media connectivity was established via supported interface Ability to enter PIN on protected media before acquisition was successful
Results:	

Assertion & Expected Result	Actual Result
A_SIM-23 SIM connectivity via supported interfaces.	as expected
A_SIM-26 Password entry before acquisition for protected SIMs.	as expected

Analysis:	Expected results achieved

5.2.23   CFT-SIM-05   (T-Mobile SIM)

Test Case CFT-SIM-05 Micro Systemation .XRY Version 3.6	
Case Summary:	CFT-SIM-05 Acquire SIM internal memory and review reported data via the preview-pane or generated reports for readability.
Assertions:	A_SIM-23 If a cellular forensic tool provides support for connectivity of the target SIM then the tool shall successfully recognize the target SIM via all vendor supported interfaces (e.g., PC/SC reader, proprietary reader). A_SIM-27 If a cellular forensic tool successfully completes acquisition of the target SIM then the tool shall have the ability to present acquired data in a human-readable format via either preview-pane or generated report.
Tester Name:	rpa
Test Host:	Morrisy
Test Date:	Thu Apr 3 12:47:19 EDT 2008
Device:	TMOBILE_SIM
Source Setup:	OS: WIN XP Interface: USB

DATA OBJECTS	DATA ELEMENTS
Abbreviated Dialing Numbers (ADN)	
	Maximum Length
	Special Character
	Blank Name
	Regular Length - Deleted Number
	Foreign Entry
Call Logs	
	Last Numbers Dialed (LND)
Text Messages	
	Incoming SMS - Read
	Incoming SMS - Foreign
	Incoming SMS - Deleted
	Incoming SMS - Unread
	Incoming Foreign EMS - Read
	Incoming EMS - Deleted

Log Highlights:	Created By .XRY Version 3.6 Acquisition started: Thu Apr 3 12:47:19 EDT 2008 Acquisition finished: Thu Apr 3 12:48:10 EDT 2008 Media connectivity was established via supported interface Readability and completeness of acquired data was successful
Results:	

Assertion & Expected Result	Actual Result
A_SIM-23 SIM connectivity via supported interfaces.	as expected
A_SIM-27 Readability and completeness of acquired data via supported reports.	as expected

Analysis:	Expected results achieved

5.2.24   CFT-SIM-06   (T-Mobile SIM)

Test Case CFT-SIM-06 Micro Systemation .XRY Version 3.6	
Case Summary:	CFT-SIM-06 Acquire SIM internal memory and review reported subscriber and equipment related information (i.e., SPN, ICCID, IMSI, MSISDN).
Assertions:	A_SIM-23 If a cellular forensic tool provides support for connectivity of the target SIM then the tool shall successfully recognize the target SIM via all vendor supported interfaces (e.g., PC/SC reader, proprietary reader). A_SIM-27 If a cellular forensic tool successfully completes acquisition of the target SIM then the tool shall have the ability to present acquired data in a human-readable format via either preview-pane or generated report. A_SIM-28 If a cellular forensic tool successfully completes acquisition of the target SIM then the SPN shall be presented in a human-readable format without modification. A_SIM-29 If a cellular forensic tool successfully completes acquisition of the target SIM then the ICCID shall be presented in a human-readable format without modification. A_SIM-30 If a cellular forensic tool successfully completes acquisition of the target SIM then the IMSI shall be presented in a human-readable format without modification. A_SIM-31 If a cellular forensic tool successfully completes acquisition of the target SIM then the MSISDN shall be presented in a human-readable format without modification.
Tester Name:	rpa
Test Host:	Morrisy
Test Date:	Thu Apr 3 12:49:21 EDT 2008
Device:	TMOBILE SIM
Source Setup:	OS: WIN XP Interface: USB

DATA OBJECTS	DATA ELEMENTS
Abbreviated Dialing Numbers (ADN)	
	Maximum Length
	Special Character
	Blank Name
	Regular Length - Deleted Number
	Foreign Entry
Call Logs	
	Last Numbers Dialed (LND)
Text Messages	
	Incoming SMS - Read
	Incoming SMS - Foreign
	Incoming SMS - Deleted
	Incoming SMS - Unread
	Incoming Foreign EMS - Read
	Incoming EMS - Deleted

Log Highlights:	Created By .XRY Version 3.6 Acquisition started: Thu Apr 3 12:49:21 EDT 2008 Acquisition finished: Thu Apr 3 12:52:03 EDT 2008 Media connectivity was established via supported interface Readability and completeness of acquired data was successful All subscriber-related data (i.e., SPN, ICCID, IMSI, MSISDN) was acquired

Results:		

Assertion & Expected Result	Actual Result
A_SIM-23 SIM connectivity via supported interfaces.	as expected
A_SIM-27 Readability and completeness of acquired data via supported reports.	as expected
A_SIM-28 Acquisition of SPN.	as expected
A_SIM-29 Acquisition of ICCID.	as expected
A_SIM-30 Acquisition of IMSI.	as expected

Test Case CFT-SIM-06 Micro Systemation .XRY Version 3.6		
	A SIM-31 Acquisition of MSISDN.	as expected
Analysis:	Expected results achieved	

5.2.25   CFT-SIM-07   (T-Mobile SIM)

Test Case CFT-SIM-07 Micro Systemation .XRY Version 3.6	
Case Summary:	CFT-SIM-07 Acquire SIM internal memory and review reported Abbreviated Dialing Numbers (ADNs).
Assertions:	A_SIM-23 If a cellular forensic tool provides support for connectivity of the target SIM then the tool shall successfully recognize the target SIM via all vendor supported interfaces (e.g., PC/SC reader, proprietary reader). A_SIM-27 If a cellular forensic tool successfully completes acquisition of the target SIM then the tool shall have the ability to present acquired data in a human-readable format via either preview-pane or generated report. A_SIM-32 If a cellular forensic tool successfully completes acquisition of the target SIM then all Abbreviated Dialing Numbers (ADN) shall be presented in a human-readable format without modification.
Tester Name:	rpa
Test Host:	Morrisy
Test Date:	Thu Apr 3 12:58:47 EDT 2008
Device:	TMOBILE SIM
Source Setup:	OS: WIN XP Interface: USB

DATA OBJECTS	DATA ELEMENTS
Abbreviated Dialing Numbers (ADN)	
	Maximum Length
	Special Character
	Blank Name
	Regular Length - Deleted Number
	Foreign Entry
Call Logs	
	Last Numbers Dialed (LND)
Text Messages	
	Incoming SMS - Read
	Incoming SMS - Foreign
	Incoming SMS - Deleted
	Incoming SMS - Unread
	Incoming Foreign EMS - Read
	Incoming EMS - Deleted

Log Highlights:	Created By .XRY Version 3.6 Acquisition started: Thu Apr 3 12:58:47 EDT 2008 Acquisition finished: Thu Apr 3 13:02:16 EDT 2008 Media connectivity was established via supported interface Readability and completeness of acquired data was successful All ADNs were acquired
Results:	

Assertion & Expected Result	Actual Result
A SIM-23 SIM connectivity via supported interfaces.	as expected
A_SIM-27 Readability and completeness of acquired data via supported reports.	as expected
A_SIM-32 Acquisition of ADNs.	as expected

Analysis:	Expected results achieved

5.2.26 CFT-SIM-08 (T-Mobile SIM)

Test Case CFT-SIM-08 Micro Systemation .XRY Version 3.6	
Case Summary:	CFT-SIM-08 Acquire SIM internal memory and review reported Last Numbers Dialed (LND).
Assertions:	A_SIM-23 If a cellular forensic tool provides support for connectivity of the target SIM then the tool shall successfully recognize the target SIM via all vendor supported interfaces (e.g., PC/SC reader, proprietary reader). A_SIM-27 If a cellular forensic tool successfully completes acquisition of the target SIM then the tool shall have the ability to present acquired data in a human-readable format via either preview-pane or generated report. A_SIM-33 If a cellular forensic tool successfully completes acquisition of the target SIM then all Last Numbers Dialed (LND) shall be presented in a human-readable format without modification.
Tester Name:	rpa
Test Host:	Morrisy
Test Date:	Thu Apr 3 13:03:20 EDT 2008
Device:	TMOBILE SIM
Source Setup:	OS: WIN XP Interface: USB

DATA OBJECTS	DATA ELEMENTS
Abbreviated Dialing Numbers (ADN)	
	Maximum Length
	Special Character
	Blank Name
	Regular Length - Deleted Number
	Foreign Entry
Call Logs	
	Last Numbers Dialed (LND)
Text Messages	
	Incoming SMS - Read
	Incoming SMS - Foreign
	Incoming SMS - Deleted
	Incoming SMS - Unread
	Incoming Foreign EMS - Read
	Incoming EMS - Deleted

Log Highlights:	Created By .XRY Version 3.6 Acquisition started: Thu Apr 3 13:03:20 EDT 2008 Acquisition finished: Thu Apr 3 13:04:13 EDT 2008 Media connectivity was established via supported interface Readability and completeness of acquired data was successful LNDs were acquired
Results:	

Assertion & Expected Result	Actual Result
A SIM-23 SIM connectivity via supported interfaces.	as expected
A_SIM-27 Readability and completeness of acquired data via supported reports.	as expected
A SIM-33 Acquisition of LNDs.	as expected

Analysis:	Expected results achieved

5.2.27   CFT-SIM-09   (T-Mobile SIM)

Test Case CFT-SIM-09 Micro Systemation .XRY Version 3.6	
Case Summary:	CFT-SIM-09 Acquire SIM internal memory and review reported text messages (i.e., SMS, EMS).
Assertions:	A_SIM-23 If a cellular forensic tool provides support for connectivity of the target SIM then the tool shall successfully recognize the target SIM via all vendor supported interfaces (e.g., PC/SC reader, proprietary reader). A_SIM-27 If a cellular forensic tool successfully completes acquisition of the target SIM then the tool shall have the ability to present acquired data in a human-readable format via either preview-pane or generated report. A_SIM-34 If a cellular forensic tool successfully completes acquisition of the target SIM then all SMS text messages shall be presented in a human-readable format without modification. A_SIM-35 If a cellular forensic tool successfully completes acquisition of the target SIM then all EMS text messages shall be presented in a human-readable format without modification.
Tester Name:	rpa
Test Host:	Morrisy
Test Date:	Thu Apr 3 13:05:15 EDT 2008
Device:	TMOBILE SIM
Source Setup:	OS: WIN XP Interface: USB

DATA OBJECTS	DATA ELEMENTS
Abbreviated Dialing Numbers (ADN)	
	Maximum Length
	Special Character
	Blank Name
	Regular Length - Deleted Number
	Foreign Entry
Call Logs	
	Last Numbers Dialed (LND)
Text Messages	
	Incoming SMS - Read
	Incoming SMS - Foreign
	Incoming SMS - Deleted
	Incoming SMS - Unread
	Incoming Foreign EMS - Read
	Incoming EMS - Deleted

Log Highlights:	Created By .XRY Version 3.6 Acquisition started: Thu Apr 3 13:05:15 EDT 2008 Acquisition finished: Thu Apr 3 13:06:41 EDT 2008 Media connectivity was established via supported interface Readability and completeness of acquired data was successful ALL text messages (SMS, EMS) were acquired

Results:

Assertion & Expected Result	Actual Result
A_SIM-23 SIM connectivity via supported interfaces.	as expected
A_SIM-27 Readability and completeness of acquired data via supported reports.	as expected
A_SIM-34 Acquisition of SMS messages.	as expected
A_SIM-35 Acquisition of EMS messages.	as expected

Analysis:	Expected results achieved

5.2.28   CFT-SIM-10   (T-Mobile SIM)

Test Case CFT-SIM-10 Micro Systemation .XRY Version 3.6	
Case Summary:	CFT-SIM-10 Acquire SIM internal memory and review reported location related data (i.e., LOCI, GPRSLOCI).
Assertions:	A_SIM-23 If a cellular forensic tool provides support for connectivity of the target SIM then the tool shall successfully recognize the target SIM via all vendor supported interfaces (e.g., PC/SC reader, proprietary reader). A_SIM-27 If a cellular forensic tool successfully completes acquisition of the target SIM then the tool shall have the ability to present acquired data in a human-readable format via either preview-pane or generated report. A_SIM-36 If a cellular forensic tool successfully completes acquisition of the target SIM then all location related data (i.e., LOCI) shall be presented in a human-readable format without modification. A_SIM-37 If a cellular forensic tool successfully completes acquisition of the target SIM then all location related data (i.e., GRPSLOCI) shall be presented in a human-readable format without modification.
Tester Name:	rpa
Test Host:	Morrisy
Test Date:	Thu Apr 3 13:07:17 EDT 2008
Device:	TMOBILE SIM
Source Setup:	OS: WIN XP Interface: USB

DATA OBJECTS	DATA ELEMENTS
Abbreviated Dialing Numbers (ADN)	
	Maximum Length
	Special Character
	Blank Name
	Regular Length - Deleted Number
	Foreign Entry
Call Logs	
	Last Numbers Dialed (LND)
Text Messages	
	Incoming SMS - Read
	Incoming SMS - Foreign
	Incoming SMS - Deleted
	Incoming SMS - Unread
	Incoming Foreign EMS - Read
	Incoming EMS - Deleted

Log Highlights:	Created By .XRY Version 3.6 Acquisition started: Thu Apr 3 13:07:17 EDT 2008 Acquisition finished: Thu Apr 3 13:08:37 EDT 2008 Media connectivity was established via supported interface Readability and completeness of acquired data was successful LOCI data was acquired GPRSLOCI data was acquired

Results:		
	Assertion & Expected Result	**Actual Result**
	A_SIM-23 SIM connectivity via supported interfaces.	as expected
	A_SIM-27 Readability and completeness of acquired data via supported reports.	as expected
	A_SIM-36 Acquisition of LOCI information.	as expected
	A_SIM-37 Acquisition of GPRSLOCI information.	as expected

Analysis:	Expected results achieved

5.2.29   CFT-SIMO-01   (T-Mobile SIM)

Test Case CFT-SIMO-01 Micro Systemation .XRY Version 3.6	
Case Summary:	CFT-SIMO-01 Acquire SIM internal memory and review acquired data via suported generated report formats.
Assertions:	A_SIMO-58 If a cellular forensic tool successfully completes acquisition of the target media (i.e., SIM) then the tool shall present the acquired data in a human-readable format without modification via supported generated report formats.
Tester Name:	rpa
Test Host:	Morrisy
Test Date:	Fri Apr 4 09:34:17 EDT 2008
Device:	TMOBILE SIM
Source Setup:	OS: WIN XP Interface: USB

DATA OBJECTS	DATA ELEMENTS
Abbreviated Dialing Numbers (ADN)	
	Maximum Length
	Special Character
	Blank Name
	Regular Length - Deleted Number
	Foreign Entry
Call Logs	
	Last Numbers Dialed (LND)
Text Messages	
	Incoming SMS - Read
	Incoming SMS - Foreign
	Incoming SMS - Deleted
	Incoming SMS - Unread
	Incoming Foreign EMS - Read
	Incoming EMS - Deleted

Log Highlights:	Created By .XRY Version 3.6 Acquisition started: Fri Apr 4 09:34:17 EDT 2008 Acquisition finished: Fri Apr 4 09:38:27 EDT 2008 Complete representation of known data via generated reports was successful

Results:	

Assertion & Expected Result	Actual Result
A_SIMO-58 Comparison of known SIM data elements via generated reports.	as expected

Analysis:	Expected results achieved

5.2.30   CFT-SIMO-02   (T-Mobile SIM)

Test Case CFT-SIMO-02 Micro Systemation .XRY Version 3.6	
Case Summary:	CFT-SIMO-02 Acquire SIM internal memory and review acquired data via the preview-pane.
Assertions:	A_SIMO-59 If a cellular forensic tool successfully completes acquisition of the target media (i.e., SIM) then the tool shall present the acquired data in a human-readable format without modification via supported generated report formats.
Tester Name:	rpa
Test Host:	Morrisy
Test Date:	Fri Apr 4 09:43:50 EDT 2008
Device:	TMOBILE SIM
Source Setup:	OS: WIN XP Interface: USB

DATA OBJECTS	DATA ELEMENTS
Abbreviated Dialing Numbers (ADN)	
	Maximum Length
	Special Character
	Blank Name
	Regular Length - Deleted Number
	Foreign Entry
Call Logs	
	Last Numbers Dialed (LND)
Text Messages	
	Incoming SMS - Read
	Incoming SMS - Foreign
	Incoming SMS - Deleted
	Incoming SMS - Unread
	Incoming Foreign EMS - Read
	Incoming EMS - Deleted

Log Highlights:	Created By .XRY Version 3.6 Acquisition started: Fri Apr 4 09:43:50 EDT 2008 Acquisition finished: Fri Apr 4 09:44:54 EDT 2008 Complete representation of known data via preview-pane was successful

Results:

Assertion & Expected Result	Actual Result
A_SIMO-59 Comparison of known SIM data elements via preview-pane.	as expected

Analysis:	Expected results achieved

5.2.31   CFT-SIMO-03   (T-Mobile SIM)

Test Case CFT-SIMO-03 Micro Systemation .XRY Version 3.6	
Case Summary:	CFT-SIMO-03 Acquire SIM internal memory and compare acquired data via the preview-pane and supported generated reports.
Assertions:	A_SIMO-58 If a cellular forensic tool successfully completes acquisition of the target media (i.e., SIM) then the tool shall present the acquired data in a human-readable format without modification via supported generated report formats. A_SIMO-59 If a cellular forensic tool successfully completes acquisition of the target media (i.e., SIM) then the tool shall present the acquired data in a human-readable format without modification via supported generated report formats. A_SIMO-60 If a cellular forensic tool provides a preview-pane view and a generated report of the acquired data then the reports shall maintain consistency of all reported data elements.
Tester Name:	rpa
Test Host:	Morrisy
Test Date:	Fri Apr 4 09:56:06 EDT 2008
Device:	TMOBILE SIM
Source Setup:	OS: WIN XP Interface: USB

DATA OBJECTS	DATA ELEMENTS
Abbreviated Dialing Numbers (ADN)	
	Maximum Length
	Special Character
	Blank Name
	Regular Length - Deleted Number
	Foreign Entry
Call Logs	
	Last Numbers Dialed (LND)
Text Messages	
	Incoming SMS - Read
	Incoming SMS - Foreign
	Incoming SMS - Deleted
	Incoming SMS - Unread
	Incoming Foreign EMS - Read
	Incoming EMS - Deleted

Log Highlights:	Created By .XRY Version 3.6 Acquisition started: Fri Apr 4 09:56:06 EDT 2008 Acquisition finished: Fri Apr 4 09:59:10 EDT 2008 Complete representation of known data via generated reports was successful Complete representation of known data via preview-pane was successful
Results:	

Assertion & Expected Result	Actual Result
A_SIMO-58 Comparison of known SIM data elements via generated reports.	as expected
A_SIMO-59 Comparison of known SIM data elements via preview-pane.	as expected
A_SIMO-60 Compare generated reports and preview-pane views for SIM acquisition.	as expected

Analysis:	Expected results achieved

5.2.32   CFT-SIMO-04   (T-Mobile SIM)

Test Case CFT-SIMO-04 Micro Systemation .XRY Version 3.6	
Case Summary:	CFT-SIMO-04 After a successful SIM internal memory acquisition, aflter the case file via third party means and attempt to re-open the case.
Assertions:	A_SIMO-61 If modification is attempted to the case file or individual data elements via third-party means then the tool shall provide protection mechanisms disallowing or reporting data modification.
Tester Name:	rpa
Test Host:	Morrisy
Test Date:	Fri Apr 4 10:00:20 EDT 2008
Device:	TMOBILE SIM

Source Setup:	OS: WIN XP Interface: USB

DATA OBJECTS	DATA ELEMENTS
Abbreviated Dialing Numbers (ADN)	
	Maximum Length
	Special Character
	Blank Name
	Regular Length - Deleted Number
	Foreign Entry
Call Logs	
	Last Numbers Dialed (LND)
Text Messages	
	Incoming SMS - Read
	Incoming SMS - Foreign
	Incoming SMS - Deleted
	Incoming SMS - Unread
	Incoming Foreign EMS - Read
	Incoming EMS - Deleted

Log Highlights:	Created By .XRY Version 3.6 Acquisition started: Fri Apr 4 10:00:20 EDT 2008 Acquisition finished: Fri Apr 4 10:01:43 EDT 2008 Notification of modified case data was successful **Notes**: Case File Encryption has to be selected before Acquisition

Results:		

Assertion & Expected Result	Actual Result
A_SIMO-61 Notification of modifod SIM case data.	as expected

Analysis:	Expected results achieved

5.2.33　　CFT-SIMO-05　　(T-Mobile SIM)

Test Case CFT-SIMO-05 Micro Systemation .XRY Version 3.6	
Case Summary:	CFT-SIMO-05 Acquire SIM internal memory and review reports for recoverable deleted data.
Assertions:	A_SIMO-58 If a cellular forensic tool successfully completes acquisition of the target media (i.e., SIM) then the tool shall present the acquired data in a human-readable format without modification via supported generated report formats. A_SIMO-59 If a cellular forensic tool successfully completes acquisition of the target media (i.e., SIM) then the tool shall present the acquired data in a human-readable format without modification via supported generated report formats. A_SIMO-62 If the cellular forensic tool successfully completes acquisition of the target SIM and recoverable deleted SMS messages exist then the tool shall present recoverable deleted data in a human-readable format without modification. A_SIMO-63 If the cellular forensic tool successfully completes acquisition of the target SIM and recoverable deleted EMS messages exist then the tool shall present recoverable deleted data in a human-readable format without modification.
Tester Name:	rpa
Test Host:	Morrisy
Test Date:	Fri Apr 4 10:23:58 EDT 2008
Device:	TMOBILE_SIM
Source Setup:	OS: WIN XP Interface: USB

DATA OBJECTS	DATA ELEMENTS
Abbreviated Dialing Numbers (ADN)	
	Maximum Length
	Special Character
	Blank Name
	Regular Length - Deleted Number
	Foreign Entry
Call Logs	
	Last Numbers Dialed (LND)
Text Messages	
	Incoming SMS - Read
	Incoming SMS - Foreign
	Incoming SMS - Deleted
	Incoming SMS - Unread
	Incoming Foreign EMS - Read
	Incoming EMS - Deleted

Log Highlights:	Created By .XRY Version 3.6 Acquisition started: Fri Apr 4 10:23:58 EDT 2008 Acquisition finished: Fri Apr 4 10:25:08 EDT 2008 Complete representation of known data via generated reports was successful Complete representation of known data via preview-pane was successful Deleted SMS data was recovered Deleted EMS data was recovered
Results:	

Assertion & Expected Result	Actual Result
A_SIMO-58 Comparison of known SIM data elements via generated reports.	as expected
A_SIMO-59 Comparison of known SIM data elements via preview-pane.	as expected
A_SIMO-62 Recovery of deleted SMS messages.	as expected
A_SIMO-63 Recovery of deleted EMS messages.	as expected

Test Case CFT-SIMO-05 Micro Systemation .XRY Version 3.6	
Analysis:	Expected results achieved

5.2.34   CFT-SIMO-06   (T-Mobile SIM)

Test Case CFT-SIMO-06 Micro Systemation .XRY Version 3.6	
Case Summary:	CFT-SIMO-06 Acquire SIM internal memory and review generated log files.
Assertions:	A_SIMO-64 If a cellular forensic tool supports creation of log files then the application should present the log files in a human-readable format outlining the acquisition process.
Tester Name:	rpa
Test Host:	Morrisy
Test Date:	Fri Apr 4 10:40:22 EDT 2008
Device:	TMOBILE SIM
Source Setup:	OS: WIN XP Interface: USB

DATA OBJECTS	DATA ELEMENTS
Abbreviated Dialing Numbers (ADN)	
	Maximum Length
	Special Character
	Blank Name
	Regular Length - Deleted Number
	Foreign Entry
Call Logs	
	Last Numbers Dialed (LND)
Text Messages	
	Incoming SMS - Read
	Incoming SMS - Foreign
	Incoming SMS - Deleted
	Incoming SMS - Unread
	Incoming Foreign EMS - Read
	Incoming EMS - Deleted

Log Highlights:	Created By .XRY Version 3.6 Acquisition started: Fri Apr 4 10:40:22 EDT 2008 Acquisition finished: Fri Apr 4 10:43:03 EDT 2008 Creation of complete and human-readable log files was successful **Notes**: XRY Log

Module	Status	Message
MAIN	Success	Initiating Process
MAIN	Success	.XRY Version 3.6
MAIN	Success	Connected to OMNIKEY CardMan 6121 0 []
MAIN	Success	Device Name: SIM Card
MAIN	Success	Starting process of SIM (3.6)
SIM	Success	Connecting
SIM	Success	Connected with T0 Protocol
SIM	Success	Detecting SIM type
SIM	Success	Identified as SIM Card
SIM	Success	Passed PIN code
SIM	Success	Analyzing MF folder
SIM	Success	Reading General Information
SIM	Success	Reading General Information
SIM	Success	Analyzing GSM Folder
SIM	Success	Reading General Information
SIM	Success	Reading Network Information
SIM	Success	Reading Network Information PLMN Selector
SIM	Success	Reading Network Information Forbidden PLMNs
SIM	Success	Analyzing Telecom Folder
SIM	Success	Reading SMS
SIM	Success	Read 30 positions, 13 used
SIM	Success	Reading General Information (MSISDN numbers)

Test Case CFT-SIMO-06 Micro Systemation .XRY Version 3.6			
	SIM	Success	Read 4 positions, 1 used
	SIM	Success	Reading Network Information
	SIM	Success	Reading Contacts
	SIM	Success	Read 250 positions, 10 used
	SIM	Success	Reading Contacts (fixed numbers)
	SIM	Success	Read 15 positions, 0 used
	SIM	Success	Reading Calls (last dialled)
	SIM	Success	Read 10 positions, 3 used
	SIM	Success	Attempting to read 02 IMEI
	SIM	Success	No IMEI Found
	MAIN	Success	SIM (3.6) completed successfully
	MAIN	Success	Processing completed successfully.
	MAIN	Success	Total processing time: 0 minutes, 7 seconds
	MAIN	Success	9 items read to General Information folder
	MAIN	Success	10 items read to Contacts folder
	MAIN	Success	3 items read to Calls folder
	MAIN	Success	12 items read to SMS folder
	MAIN	Success	13 items read to Network Information folder

Results:		
	Assertion & Expected Result	**Actual Result**
	A SIMO-64 SIM log file output.	as expected

Analysis:	Expected results achieved

5.2.35   CFT-SIMO-07   (T-Mobile SIM)

Test Case CFT-SIMO-07 Micro Systemation .XRY Version 3.6	
Case Summary:	CFT-SIMO-07 Acquire SIM internal memory and review data containing foreign language characters.
Assertions:	A_SIMO-58 If a cellular forensic tool successfully completes acquisition of the target media (i.e., SIM) then the tool shall present the acquired data in a human-readable format without modification via supported generated report formats. A_SIMO-59 If a cellular forensic tool successfully completes acquisition of the target media (i.e., SIM) then the tool shall present the acquired data in a human-readable format without modification via supported generated report formats. A_SIMO-65 If the cellular forensic tool supports proper display of foreign language character sets then the application should present abbreviated dialing numbers (ADNs) containing foreign language characters in their native format without modification. A_SIMO-66 If the cellular forensic tool supports proper display of foreign language character sets then the application should present text messages containing foreign language characters in their native format without modification.
Tester Name:	rpa
Test Host:	Morrisy
Test Date:	Fri Apr 4 12:43:30 EDT 2008
Device:	TMOBILE SIM
Source Setup:	OS: WIN XP Interface: USB

DATA OBJECTS	DATA ELEMENTS
Abbreviated Dialing Numbers (ADN)	
	Maximum Length
	Special Character
	Blank Name
	Regular Length - Deleted Number
	Foreign Entry
Call Logs	
	Last Numbers Dialed (LND)
Text Messages	
	Incoming SMS - Read
	Incoming SMS - Foreign
	Incoming SMS - Deleted
	Incoming SMS - Unread
	Incoming Foreign EMS - Read
	Incoming EMS - Deleted

Log Highlights:	Created By .XRY Version 3.6 Acquisition started: Fri Apr 4 12:43:30 EDT 2008 Acquisition finished: Fri Apr 4 12:44:21 EDT 2008 Complete representation of known data via generated reports was successful Complete representation of known data via preview-pane was successful ADNs containing foreign characters were acquired and properly displayed Text messages containing foreign characters were acquired and properly displayed
Results:	

Assertion & Expected Result	Actual Result
A_SIMO-58 Comparison of known SIM data elements via generated reports.	as expected
A_SIMO-59 Comparison of known SIM data elements via preview-pane.	as expected
A_SIMO-65 Acquisition of ADNs containing foreign language characters.	as expected
A_SIMO-66 Acquisition of text messages containing foreign	as expected

	language characters.	
Analysis:	Expected results achieved	

5.2.36 CFT-SIMO-08 (T-Mobile SIM)

Test Case CFT-SIMO-08 Micro Systemation .XRY Version 3.6	
Case Summary:	CFT-SIMO-08 Begin acquisition on a PIN protected SIM to determine if the tool provides an accurate count of the remaining number of PIN attempts and if the PIN attempts are decremented when entering an incorrect value.
Assertions:	A_SIMO-67 If a cellular forensic tool provides the examiner with the remaining number of authentication attempts then the application should provide an accurate count of the remaining PIN attempts.
Tester Name:	rpa
Test Host:	Morrisy
Test Date:	Fri Apr 4 12:46:34 EDT 2008
Device:	TMOBILE SIM
Source Setup:	OS: WIN XP Interface: USB

DATA OBJECTS	DATA ELEMENTS
Abbreviated Dialing Numbers (ADN)	
	Maximum Length
	Special Character
	Blank Name
	Regular Length - Deleted Number
	Foreign Entry
Call Logs	
	Last Numbers Dialed (LND)
Text Messages	
	Incoming SMS - Read
	Incoming SMS - Foreign
	Incoming SMS - Deleted
	Incoming SMS - Unread
	Incoming Foreign EMS - Read
	Incoming EMS - Deleted

Log Highlights:	Created By .XRY Version 3.6 Acquisition started: Fri Apr 4 12:46:34 EDT 2008 Acquisition finished: Fri Apr 4 12:48:08 EDT 2008 Remaining number of PIN attempts properly displayed was successful

Results:		
	Assertion & Expected Result	**Actual Result**
	A_SIMO-67 Display of remaining number of PIN attempts.	as expected

Analysis:	Expected results achieved

5.2.37   CFT-SIMO-09   (T-Mobile SIM)

Test Case CFT-SIMO-09 Micro Systemation .XRY Version 3.6	
Case Summary:	CFT-SIMO-09 Begin acquisition on a SIM whose PIN attempts have been exhausted to determine if the tool provides an accurate count of the remaining number of PUK attempts and if the PUK attempts are decremented when entering an incorrect value.
Assertions:	A_SIMO-68 If a cellular forensic tool provides the examiner with the remaining number of PUK attempts then the application should provide an accurate count of the remaining PUK attempts.
Tester Name:	rpa
Test Host:	Morrisy
Test Date:	Fri Apr 4 14:11:34 EDT 2008
Device:	TMOBILE SIM
Source Setup:	OS: WIN XP Interface: USB

DATA OBJECTS	DATA ELEMENTS
Abbreviated Dialing Numbers (ADN)	
	Maximum Length
	Special Character
	Blank Name
	Regular Length - Deleted Number
	Foreign Entry
Call Logs	
	Last Numbers Dialed (LND)
Text Messages	
	Incoming SMS - Read
	Incoming SMS - Foreign
	Incoming SMS - Deleted
	Incoming SMS - Unread
	Incoming Foreign EMS - Read
	Incoming EMS - Deleted

Log Highlights:	Created By .XRY Version 3.6 Acquisition started: Fri Apr 4 14:11:34 EDT 2008 Acquisition finished: Fri Apr 4 14:12:44 EDT 2008 Remaining number of PUK attempts properly displayed was successful

Results:

Assertion & Expected Result	Actual Result
A SIMO-68 Display of remaining number of PUK attempts.	as expected

Analysis:	Expected results achieved

5.2.38   CFT-IM-01   (Motorola RAZR V3)

Test Case CFT-IM-01 Micro Systemation .XRY Version 3.6	
Case Summary:	CFT-IM-01 Acquire mobile device internal memory over supported interfaces (e.g., cable, Bluetooth, IrDA).
Assertions:	A_IM-01 If a cellular forensic tool provides support for connectivity of the target device then the tool shall successfully recognize the target device via all vendor supported interfaces (e.g., cable, Bluetooth, IrDA).
Tester Name:	rpa
Test Host:	Morrisy
Test Date:	Wed Apr 9 08:12:43 EDT 2008
Device:	Motorola RAZR V3
Source Setup:	OS: WIN XP Interface: cable, Bluetooth

DATA OBJECTS	DATA ELEMENTS
Address Book Entries	
	Maximum Length
	Regular Length, email, picture
	Special Character
	Blank Name
	Regular Length, Deleted email - deleted picture
	Deleted Entry
	Foreign Entry
PIM Data	
	Maximum Length
	Regular Length
	Deleted Entry
	Special Character
Call Logs	
	Missed
	Missed - Deleted
	Incoming
	Incoming - Deleted
	Outgoing
	Outgoing - Deleted
Text Messages	
	Incoming SMS - Read
	Incoming SMS - Unread
	Incoming SMS - Deleted
	Outgoing SMS
	Outgoing SMS - Deleted
	Incoming EMS - Read
	Incoming EMS - Unread
	Incoming Foreign EMS - Read
	Incoming EMS - Deleted
	Outgoing EMS
	Outgoing EMS - Deleted
MMS Messages	
	Incoming Audio
	Incoming Image
	Incoming Video
	Outgoing Audio
	Outgoing Image
	Outgoing Video
Stand-alone data files	
	Audio
	Audio - Deleted
	Image
	Image - Deleted
	Video
	Video - Deleted

Log	Created By .XRY Version 3.6

Test Case CFT-IM-01 Micro Systemation .XRY Version 3.6	
Highlights:	Acquisition started: Wed Apr 9 08:12:43 EDT 2008 Acquisition finished: Wed Apr 9 08:19:21 EDT 2008 Device connectivity was established via supported interface (i.e., cable, Bluetooth) **Notes**: IrDA acquisition not supported.
Results:	

Assertion & Expected Result	Actual Result
A_IM-01 Device connectivity via supported interfaces.	as expected

Analysis:	Expected results achieved

5.2.39   CFT-IM-02 (Motorola RAZR V3)

Test Case CFT-IM-02 Micro Systemation .XRY Version 3.6	
Case Summary:	CFT-IM-02 Attempt internal memory acquisition of a non-supported mobile device.
Assertions:	A_IM-02 If a cellular forensic tool attempts to connect to a non-supported device then the tool shall have the ability to identify that the device is not supported.
Tester Name:	rpa
Test Host:	Morrisy
Test Date:	Wed Apr 9 08:24:21 EDT 2008
Device:	non-supported mobile device
Source Setup:	OS: WIN XP Interface: cable

DATA OBJECTS	DATA ELEMENTS
Address Book Entries	
	Maximum Length
	Regular Length, email, picture
	Special Character
	Blank Name
	Regular Length, Deleted email - deleted picture
	Deleted Entry
	Foreign Entry
PIM Data	
	Maximum Length
	Regular Length
	Deleted Entry
	Special Character
Call Logs	
	Missed
	Missed - Deleted
	Incoming
	Incoming - Deleted
	Outgoing
	Outgoing - Deleted
Text Messages	
	Incoming SMS - Read
	Incoming SMS - Unread
	Incoming SMS - Deleted
	Outgoing SMS
	Outgoing SMS - Deleted
	Incoming EMS - Read
	Incoming EMS - Unread
	Incoming Foreign EMS - Read
	Incoming EMS - Deleted
	Outgoing EMS
	Outgoing EMS - Deleted
MMS Messages	
	Incoming Audio
	Incoming Image
	Incoming Video
	Outgoing Audio
	Outgoing Image
	Outgoing Video
Stand-alone data files	
	Audio
	Audio - Deleted
	Image
	Image - Deleted
	Video
	Video - Deleted

Log	Created By .XRY Version 3.6

Test Case CFT-IM-02 Micro Systemation .XRY Version 3.6	
Highlights:	Acquisition started: Wed Apr 9 08:24:21 EDT 2008 Acquisition finished: Wed Apr 9 08:26:27 EDT 2008 Identification of non-supported devices was successful
Results:	

Assertion & Expected Result	Actual Result
A IM-02 Identification of non-supported devices.	as expected

Analysis:	Expected results achieved

5.2.40   CFT-IM-03 (Motorola RAZR V3)

Test Case CFT-IM-03 Micro Systemation .XRY Version 3.6	
Case Summary:	CFT-IM-03 Begin mobile device internal memory acquisition and interrupt connectivity by interface disengagement.
Assertions:	A_IM-01 If a cellular forensic tool provides support for connectivity of the target device then the tool shall successfully recognize the target device via all vendor supported interfaces (e.g., cable, Bluetooth, IrDA). A_IM-03 If a cellular forensic tool encounters disengagement between the device and application then the application shall notify the user that connectivity has been disrupted.
Tester Name:	rpa
Test Host:	Morrisy
Test Date:	Wed Apr 9 08:34:52 EDT 2008
Device:	Motorola_RAZR_V3
Source Setup:	OS: WIN XP Interface: cable

DATA OBJECTS	DATA ELEMENTS
Address Book Entries	
	Maximum Length
	Regular Length, email, picture
	Special Character
	Blank Name
	Regular Length, Deleted email - deleted picture
	Deleted Entry
	Foreign Entry
PIM Data	
	Maximum Length
	Regular Length
	Deleted Entry
	Special Character
Call Logs	
	Missed
	Missed - Deleted
	Incoming
	Incoming - Deleted
	Outgoing
	Outgoing - Deleted
Text Messages	
	Incoming SMS - Read
	Incoming SMS - Unread
	Incoming SMS - Deleted
	Outgoing SMS
	Outgoing SMS - Deleted
	Incoming EMS - Read
	Incoming EMS - Unread
	Incoming Foreign EMS - Read
	Incoming EMS - Deleted
	Outgoing EMS
	Outgoing EMS - Deleted
MMS Messages	
	Incoming Audio
	Incoming Image
	Incoming Video
	Outgoing Audio
	Outgoing Image
	Outgoing Video
Stand-alone data files	
	Audio
	Audio - Deleted
	Image
	Image - Deleted
	Video
	Video - Deleted

Test Case CFT-IM-03 Micro Systemation .XRY Version 3.6	
Log Highlights:	Created By .XRY Version 3.6 Acquisition started: Wed Apr 9 08:34:52 EDT 2008 Acquisition finished: Wed Apr 9 08:35:24 EDT 2008 Device connectivity was established via supported interface Device acquisition disruption notification was successful
Results:	

Assertion & Expected Result	Actual Result
A_IM-01 Device connectivity via supported interfaces.	as expected
A_IM-03 Notification of device acquisition disruption.	as expected

Analysis:	Expected results achieved

5.2.41   CFT-IM-04 (Motorola RAZR V3)

Test Case CFT-IM-04 Micro Systemation .XRY Version 3.6	
Case Summary:	CFT-IM-04 Acquire mobile device internal memory and review reported data via the preview-pane or generated reports for readability.
Assertions:	A_IM-01 If a cellular forensic tool provides support for connectivity of the target device then the tool shall successfully recognize the target device via all vendor supported interfaces (e.g., cable, Bluetooth, IrDA). A_IM-04 If a cellular forensic tool successfully completes acquisition of the target device then the tool shall have the ability to present acquired data elements in a human-readable format via either a preview-pane or generated report.
Tester Name:	rpa
Test Host:	Morrisy
Test Date:	Wed Apr 9 08:37:15 EDT 2008
Device:	Motorola_RAZR_V3
Source Setup:	OS: WIN XP Interface: cable

DATA OBJECTS	DATA ELEMENTS
Address Book Entries	
	Maximum Length
	Regular Length, email, picture
	Special Character
	Blank Name
	Regular Length, Deleted email - deleted picture
	Deleted Entry
	Foreign Entry
PIM Data	
	Maximum Length
	Regular Length
	Deleted Entry
	Special Character
Call Logs	
	Missed
	Missed - Deleted
	Incoming
	Incoming - Deleted
	Outgoing
	Outgoing - Deleted
Text Messages	
	Incoming SMS - Read
	Incoming SMS - Unread
	Incoming SMS - Deleted
	Outgoing SMS
	Outgoing SMS - Deleted
	Incoming EMS - Read
	Incoming EMS - Unread
	Incoming Foreign EMS - Read
	Incoming EMS - Deleted
	Outgoing EMS
	Outgoing EMS - Deleted
MMS Messages	
	Incoming Audio
	Incoming Image
	Incoming Video
	Outgoing Audio
	Outgoing Image
	Outgoing Video
Stand-alone data files	
	Audio
	Audio - Deleted
	Image
	Image - Deleted
	Video
	Video - Deleted

Test Case CFT-IM-04 Micro Systemation .XRY Version 3.6	
Log Highlights:	Created By .XRY Version 3.6 Acquisition started: Wed Apr 9 08:37:15 EDT 2008 Acquisition finished: Wed Apr 9 08:39:25 EDT 2008 Device connectivity was established via supported interface Readability and completeness of acquired data was successful **Notes**: Test case performed over supported Bluetooth interface produced consistent results with the cable acquisition.
Results:	

Assertion & Expected Result	Actual Result
A_IM-01 Device connectivity via supported interfaces.	as expected
A_IM-04 Readability and completeness of acquired data via supported reports.	as expected

Analysis:	Expected results achieved

5.2.42   CFT-IM-05 (Motorola RAZR V3)

Test Case CFT-IM-05 Micro Systemation .XRY Version 3.6	
Case Summary:	CFT-IM-05 Acquire mobile device internal memory and review reported subscriber and equipment related information (i.e., IMEI, MSISDN).
Assertions:	A_IM-01 If a cellular forensic tool provides support for connectivity of the target device then the tool shall successfully recognize the target device via all vendor supported interfaces (e.g., cable, Bluetooth, IrDA). A_IM-04 If a cellular forensic tool successfully completes acquisition of the target device then the tool shall have the ability to present acquired data elements in a human-readable format via either a preview-pane or generated report. A_IM-05 If a cellular forensic tool successfully completes acquisition of the target device then subscriber related information shall be presented in a human-readable format without modification. A_IM-06 If a cellular forensic tool successfully completes acquisition of the target device then equipment related information shall be presented in a human-readable format without modification.
Tester Name:	rpa
Test Host:	Morrisy
Test Date:	Wed Apr 9 08:42:29 EDT 2008
Device:	Motorola_RAZR_V3
Source Setup:	OS: WIN XP Interface: cable

DATA OBJECTS	DATA ELEMENTS
Address Book Entries	
	Maximum Length
	Regular Length, email, picture
	Special Character
	Blank Name
	Regular Length, Deleted email - deleted picture
	Deleted Entry
	Foreign Entry
PIM Data	
	Maximum Length
	Regular Length
	Deleted Entry
	Special Character
Call Logs	
	Missed
	Missed - Deleted
	Incoming
	Incoming - Deleted
	Outgoing
	Outgoing - Deleted
Text Messages	
	Incoming SMS - Read
	Incoming SMS - Unread
	Incoming SMS - Deleted
	Outgoing SMS
	Outgoing SMS - Deleted
	Incoming EMS - Read
	Incoming EMS - Unread
	Incoming Foreign EMS - Read
	Incoming EMS - Deleted
	Outgoing EMS
	Outgoing EMS - Deleted
MMS Messages	
	Incoming Audio
	Incoming Image
	Incoming Video
	Outgoing Audio
	Outgoing Image
	Outgoing Video
Stand-alone data files	

	Audio
	Audio - Deleted
	Image
	Image - Deleted
	Video
	Video - Deleted

Log Highlights:	Created By .XRY Version 3.6 Acquisition started: Wed Apr 9 08:42:29 EDT 2008 Acquisition finished: Wed Apr 9 08:45:38 EDT 2008 Device connectivity was established via supported interface Readability and completeness of acquired data was successful Subscriber and Equipment related data (i.e., MSISDN, IMEI) were acquired **Notes**: Test case performed over supported Bluetooth interface produced consistent results with the cable acquisition.

Results:

Assertion & Expected Result	Actual Result
A IM-01 Device connectivity via supported interfaces.	as expected
A_IM-04 Readability and completeness of acquired data via supported reports.	as expected
A IM-05 Acquisition of MSISDN.	as expected
A IM-06 Acquisition of IMEI.	as expected

Analysis:	Expected results achieved

5.2.43 CFT-IM-06 (Motorola RAZR V3)

Test Case CFT-IM-06 Micro Systemation .XRY Version 3.6	
Case Summary:	CFT-IM-06 Acquire mobile device internal memory and review reported PIM related data.
Assertions:	A_IM-01 If a cellular forensic tool provides support for connectivity of the target device then the tool shall successfully recognize the target device via all vendor supported interfaces (e.g., cable, Bluetooth, IrDA).
	A_IM-04 If a cellular forensic tool successfully completes acquisition of the target device then the tool shall have the ability to present acquired data elements in a human-readable format via either a preview-pane or generated report.
	A_IM-07 If a cellular forensic tool successfully completes acquisition of the target device then all known address book entries shall be presented in a human-readable format without modification.
	A_IM-08 If a cellular forensic tool successfully completes acquisition of the target device then all known maximum length address book entries shall be presented in a human-readable format without modification.
	A_IM-09 If a cellular forensic tool successfully completes acquisition of the target device then all known address book entries containing special characters shall be presented in a human-readable format without modification.
	A_IM-10 If a cellular forensic tool successfully completes acquisition of the target device then all known address book entries containing blank names shall be presented in a human-readable format without modification.
	A_IM-11 If a cellular forensic tool successfully completes acquisition of the target device then all known email addresses associated with address book entries shall be presented in a human-readable format without modification.
	A_IM-12 If a cellular forensic tool successfully completes acquisition of the target device then all known graphics associated with address book entries shall be presented in a human-readable format without modification.
	A_IM-13 If a cellular forensic tool successfully completes acquisition of the target device then all known datebook, calendar, note entries shall be presented in a human-readable format without modification.
	A_IM-14 If a cellular forensic tool successfully completes acquisition of the target device then all maximum length datebook, calendar, note entries shall be presented in a human readable format without modification.
Tester Name:	rpa
Test Host:	Morrisy
Test Date:	Wed Apr 9 08:55:23 EDT 2008
Device:	Motorola RAZR V3
Source Setup:	OS: WIN XP Interface: cable

DATA OBJECTS	DATA ELEMENTS
Address Book Entries	
	Maximum Length
	Regular Length, email, picture
	Special Character
	Blank Name
	Regular Length, Deleted email - deleted picture
	Deleted Entry
	Foreign Entry
PIM Data	
	Maximum Length
	Regular Length
	Deleted Entry
	Special Character
Call Logs	
	Missed
	Missed - Deleted
	Incoming
	Incoming - Deleted
	Outgoing
	Outgoing - Deleted
Text Messages	

	Incoming SMS - Read
	Incoming SMS - Unread
	Incoming SMS - Deleted
	Outgoing SMS
	Outgoing SMS - Deleted
	Incoming EMS - Read
	Incoming EMS - Unread
	Incoming Foreign EMS - Read
	Incoming EMS - Deleted
	Outgoing EMS
	Outgoing EMS - Deleted
MMS Messages	
	Incoming Audio
	Incoming Image
	Incoming Video
	Outgoing Audio
	Outgoing Image
	Outgoing Video
Stand-alone data files	
	Audio
	Audio - Deleted
	Image
	Image - Deleted
	Video
	Video - Deleted

Log Highlights:	Created By .XRY Version 3.6 Acquisition started: Wed Apr 9 08:55:23 EDT 2008 Acquisition finished: Wed Apr 9 09:05:15 EDT 2008 Device connectivity was established via supported interface Readability and completeness of acquired data was successful All address book entries were successfully acquired ALL PIM related data was acquired **Notes:** Test case performed over supported Bluetooth interface produced consistent results with the cable acquisition.
Results:	

Assertion & Expected Result	Actual Result
A_IM-01 Device connectivity via supported interfaces.	as expected
A_IM-04 Readability and completeness of acquired data via supported reports.	as expected
A_IM-07 Acquisition of address book entries.	as expected
A_IM-08 Acquisition of maximum length address book entries.	as expected
A_IM-09 Acquisition of address book entries containing special characters.	as expected
A_IM-10 Acquisition of address book entries containing a blank name entry.	as expected
A_IM-11 Acquisition of embedded email addresses within address book entries.	as expected
A_IM-12 Acquisition of embedded graphics within address book entries.	as expected
A_IM-13 Acquisition of PIM data (i.e., datebook/calendar, notes).	as expected
A_IM-14 Acquisition of maximum length PIM data.	as expected

Analysis:	Expected results achieved

5.2.44   CFT-IM-07 (Motorola RAZR V3)

Test Case CFT-IM-07 Micro Systemation .XRY Version 3.6	
Case Summary:	CFT-IM-07 Acquire mobile device internal memory and review reported call logs.
Assertions:	A_IM-01 If a cellular forensic tool provides support for connectivity of the target device then the tool shall successfully recognize the target device via all vendor supported interfaces (e.g., cable, Bluetooth, IrDA). A_IM-04 If a cellular forensic tool successfully completes acquisition of the target device then the tool shall have the ability to present acquired data elements in a human-readable format via either a preview-pane or generated report. A_IM-15 If a cellular forensic tool successfully completes acquisition of the target device then all call logs (incoming/outgoing) shall be presented in a human-readable format without modification.
Tester Name:	rpa
Test Host:	Morrisy
Test Date:	Wed Apr 9 10:06:46 EDT 2008
Device:	Motorola RAZR V3
Source Setup:	OS: WIN XP Interface: cable

DATA OBJECTS	DATA ELEMENTS
Address Book Entries	
	Maximum Length
	Regular Length, email, picture
	Special Character
	Blank Name
	Regular Length, Deleted email - deleted picture
	Deleted Entry
	Foreign Entry
PIM Data	
	Maximum Length
	Regular Length
	Deleted Entry
	Special Character
Call Logs	
	Missed
	Missed - Deleted
	Incoming
	Incoming - Deleted
	Outgoing
	Outgoing - Deleted
Text Messages	
	Incoming SMS - Read
	Incoming SMS - Unread
	Incoming SMS - Deleted
	Outgoing SMS
	Outgoing SMS - Deleted
	Incoming EMS - Read
	Incoming EMS - Unread
	Incoming Foreign EMS - Read
	Incoming EMS - Deleted
	Outgoing EMS
	Outgoing EMS - Deleted
MMS Messages	
	Incoming Audio
	Incoming Image
	Incoming Video
	Outgoing Audio
	Outgoing Image
	Outgoing Video
Stand-alone data files	
	Audio
	Audio - Deleted
	Image

Test Case CFT-IM-07 Micro Systemation .XRY Version 3.6	
	Image - Deleted
	Video
	Video - Deleted

Log Highlights:	Created By .XRY Version 3.6 Acquisition started: Wed Apr 9 10:06:46 EDT 2008 Acquisition finished: Wed Apr 9 10:09:01 EDT 2008 Device connectivity was established via supported interface Readability and completeness of acquired data was successful All Call Logs (incoming, outgoing) were acquired **Notes**: Test case performed over supported Bluetooth interface produced consistent results with the cable acquisition.

Results:		
	Assertion & Expected Result	**Actual Result**
	A_IM-01 Device connectivity via supported interfaces.	as expected
	A_IM-04 Readability and completeness of acquired data via supported reports.	as expected
	A_IM-15 Acquisition of call logs.	as expected

Analysis:	Expected results achieved

5.2.45   CFT-IM-08 (Motorola RAZR V3)

Test Case CFT-IM-08 Micro Systemation .XRY Version 3.6	
Case Summary:	CFT-IM-08 Acquire mobile device internal memory and review reported text messages.
Assertions:	A_IM-01 If a cellular forensic tool provides support for connectivity of the target device then the tool shall successfully recognize the target device via all vendor supported interfaces (e.g., cable, Bluetooth, IrDA). A_IM-04 If a cellular forensic tool successfully completes acquisition of the target device then the tool shall have the ability to present acquired data elements in a human-readable format via either a preview-pane or generated report. A_IM-16 If a cellular forensic tool successfully completes acquisition of the target device then all text messages (i.e., SMS, EMS) messages shall be presented in a human-readable format without modification.
Tester Name:	rpa
Test Host:	Morrisy
Test Date:	Wed Apr 9 09:35:52 EDT 2008
Device:	Motorola RAZR V3
Source Setup:	OS: WIN XP Interface: cable

DATA OBJECTS	DATA ELEMENTS
Address Book Entries	
	Maximum Length
	Regular Length, email, picture
	Special Character
	Blank Name
	Regular Length, Deleted email - deleted picture
	Deleted Entry
	Foreign Entry
PIM Data	
	Maximum Length
	Regular Length
	Deleted Entry
	Special Character
Call Logs	
	Missed
	Missed - Deleted
	Incoming
	Incoming - Deleted
	Outgoing
	Outgoing - Deleted
Text Messages	
	Incoming SMS - Read
	Incoming SMS - Unread
	Incoming SMS - Deleted
	Outgoing SMS
	Outgoing SMS - Deleted
	Incoming EMS - Read
	Incoming EMS - Unread
	Incoming Foreign EMS - Read
	Incoming EMS - Deleted
	Outgoing EMS
	Outgoing EMS - Deleted
MMS Messages	
	Incoming Audio
	Incoming Image
	Incoming Video
	Outgoing Audio
	Outgoing Image
	Outgoing Video
Stand-alone data files	
	Audio
	Audio - Deleted
	Image

Test Case CFT-IM-08 Micro Systemation .XRY Version 3.6

	Image - Deleted
	Video
	Video - Deleted

Log Highlights:	Created By .XRY Version 3.6 Acquisition started: Wed Apr 9 09:35:52 EDT 2008 Acquisition finished: Wed Apr 9 09:39:33 EDT 2008 Device connectivity was established via supported interface Readability and completeness of acquired data was successful ALL text messages (SMS, EMS) were acquired **Notes**: Test case performed over supported Bluetooth interface produced consistent results with the cable acquisition.

Results:	

Assertion & Expected Result	Actual Result
A_IM-01 Device connectivity via supported interfaces.	as expected
A_IM-04 Readability and completeness of acquired data via supported reports.	as expected
A_IM-16 Acquisition of text messages.	as expected

Analysis:	Expected results achieved

5.2.46 CFT-IM-09 (Motorola RAZR V3)

Test Case CFT-IM-09 Micro Systemation .XRY Version 3.6	
Case Summary:	CFT-IM-09 Acquire mobile device internal memory and review reported MMS multi-media related data (i.e., text, audio, graphics, video).
Assertions:	A_IM-01 If a cellular forensic tool provides support for connectivity of the target device then the tool shall successfully recognize the target device via all vendor supported interfaces (e.g., cable, Bluetooth, IrDA). A_IM-04 If a cellular forensic tool successfully completes acquisition of the target device then the tool shall have the ability to present acquired data elements in a human-readable format via either a preview-pane or generated report. A_IM-17 If a cellular forensic tool successfully completes acquisition of the target device then all MMS messages and associated audio shall be presented properly without modification. A_IM-18 If a cellular forensic tool successfully completes acquisition of the target device then all MMS messages and associated images shall be presented properly without modification. A_IM-19 If a cellular forensic tool successfully completes acquisition of the target device then all MMS messages and associated video shall be presented properly without modification.
Tester Name:	rpa
Test Host:	Morrisy
Test Date:	Wed Apr 9 09:41:47 EDT 2008
Device:	Motorola RAZR V3
Source Setup:	OS: WIN XP Interface: cable

DATA OBJECTS	DATA ELEMENTS
Address Book Entries	
	Maximum Length
	Regular Length, email, picture
	Special Character
	Blank Name
	Regular Length, Deleted email - deleted picture
	Deleted Entry
	Foreign Entry
PIM Data	
	Maximum Length
	Regular Length
	Deleted Entry
	Special Character
Call Logs	
	Missed
	Missed - Deleted
	Incoming
	Incoming - Deleted
	Outgoing
	Outgoing - Deleted
Text Messages	
	Incoming SMS - Read
	Incoming SMS - Unread
	Incoming SMS - Deleted
	Outgoing SMS
	Outgoing SMS - Deleted
	Incoming EMS - Read
	Incoming EMS - Unread
	Incoming Foreign EMS - Read
	Incoming EMS - Deleted
	Outgoing EMS
	Outgoing EMS - Deleted
MMS Messages	
	Incoming Audio
	Incoming Image
	Incoming Video

		Outgoing Audio
		Outgoing Image
		Outgoing Video
	Stand-alone data files	
		Audio
		Audio - Deleted
		Image
		Image - Deleted
		Video
		Video - Deleted

Log Highlights:	Created By .XRY Version 3.6 Acquisition started: Wed Apr 9 09:41:47 EDT 2008 Acquisition finished: Wed Apr 9 09:43:17 EDT 2008 Device connectivity was established via supported interface Readability and completeness of acquired data was successful ALL MMS messages (Audio, Image, Video) were acquired **Notes:** QuickTime Version 7.4.1 was used to execute MMS attachments. Test case performed over supported Bluetooth interface produced consistent results with the cable acquisition.

Results:		
	Assertion & Expected Result	**Actual Result**
	A IM-01 Device connectivity via supported interfaces.	as expected
	A_IM-04 Readability and completeness of acquired data via supported reports.	as expected
	A IM-17 Acquisition of audio MMS messages.	as expected
	A IM-18 Acquisition of image MMS messages.	as expected
	A_IM-19 Acquisition of video MMS messages.	as expected

Analysis:	Expected results achieved

5.2.47　CFT-IM-10　(Motorola RAZR V3)

Test Case CFT-IM-10 Micro Systemation .XRY Version 3.6	
Case Summary:	CFT-IM-10 Acquire mobile device internal memory and review reported stand-alone multi-media data (i.e., audio, graphics, video).
Assertions:	A_IM-01 If a cellular forensic tool provides support for connectivity of the target device then the tool shall successfully recognize the target device via all vendor supported interfaces (e.g., cable, Bluetooth, IrDA). A_IM-04 If a cellular forensic tool successfully completes acquisition of the target device then the tool shall have the ability to present acquired data elements in a human-readable format via either a preview-pane or generated report. A_IM-20 If a cellular forensic tool successfully completes acquisition of the target device then all stand-alone audio files shall be playable via either an internal application or suggested third-party application without modification. A_IM-21 If a cellular forensic tool successfully completes acquisition of the target device then all stand-alone image files shall be viewable via either an internal application or suggested third-party application without modification. A_IM-22 If a cellular forensic tool successfully completes acquisition of the target device then all stand-alone video files shall be viewable via either an internal application or suggested third-party application without modification.
Tester Name:	rpa
Test Host:	Morrisy
Test Date:	Wed Apr 9 10:00:13 EDT 2008
Device:	Motorola RAZR V3
Source Setup:	OS: WIN XP Interface: cable

DATA OBJECTS	DATA ELEMENTS
Address Book Entries	
	Maximum Length
	Regular Length, email, picture
	Special Character
	Blank Name
	Regular Length, Deleted email - deleted picture
	Deleted Entry
	Foreign Entry
PIM Data	
	Maximum Length
	Regular Length
	Deleted Entry
	Special Character
Call Logs	
	Missed
	Missed - Deleted
	Incoming
	Incoming - Deleted
	Outgoing
	Outgoing - Deleted
Text Messages	
	Incoming SMS - Read
	Incoming SMS - Unread
	Incoming SMS - Deleted
	Outgoing SMS
	Outgoing SMS - Deleted
	Incoming EMS - Read
	Incoming EMS - Unread
	Incoming Foreign EMS - Read
	Incoming EMS - Deleted
	Outgoing EMS
	Outgoing EMS - Deleted
MMS Messages	
	Incoming Audio

Test Case CFT-IM-10 Micro Systemation .XRY Version 3.6		
		Incoming Image
		Incoming Video
		Outgoing Audio
		Outgoing Image
		Outgoing Video
	Stand-alone data files	
		Audio
		Audio - Deleted
		Image
		Image - Deleted
		Video
		Video - Deleted

Log Highlights:	Created By .XRY Version 3.6 Acquisition started: Wed Apr 9 10:00:13 EDT 2008 Acquisition finished: Wed Apr 9 10:01:49 EDT 2008 Device connectivity was established via supported interface Readability and completeness of acquired data was successful ALL stand-alone data files (Audio, Image, Video) were acquired **Notes:** Test case performed over supported Bluetooth interface produced consistent results with the cable acquisition.

Results:

Assertion & Expected Result	Actual Result
A IM-01 Device connectivity via supported interfaces.	as expected
A_IM-04 Readability and completeness of acquired data via supported reports.	as expected
A IM-20 Acquisition of stand-alone audio files.	as expected
A IM-21 Acquisition of stand-alone graphic files.	as expected
A IM-22 Acquisition of stand-alone video files.	as expected

Analysis:	Expected results achieved

5.2.48   CFT-IMO-01   (Motorola RAZR V3)

Test Case CFT-IMO-01 Micro Systemation .XRY Version 3.6	
Case Summary:	CFT-IMO-01 Acquire mobile device internal memory and review reported data via supported generated report formats.
Assertions:	A_IMO-38 If a cellular forensic tool successfully completes acquisition of the target device then the tool shall present the acquired data without modification via supported generated report formats.
Tester Name:	rpa
Test Host:	Morrisy
Test Date:	Fri Apr 11 12:18:47 EDT 2008
Device:	Motorola RAZR V3
Source Setup:	OS: WIN XP Interface: cable

DATA OBJECTS	DATA ELEMENTS
Address Book Entries	
	Maximum Length
	Regular Length, email, picture
	Special Character
	Blank Name
	Regular Length, Deleted email - deleted picture
	Deleted Entry
	Foreign Entry
PIM Data	
	Maximum Length
	Regular Length
	Deleted Entry
	Special Character
Call Logs	
	Missed
	Missed - Deleted
	Incoming
	Incoming - Deleted
	Outgoing
	Outgoing - Deleted
Text Messages	
	Incoming SMS - Read
	Incoming SMS - Unread
	Incoming SMS - Deleted
	Outgoing SMS
	Outgoing SMS - Deleted
	Incoming EMS - Read
	Incoming EMS - Unread
	Incoming Foreign EMS - Read
	Incoming EMS - Deleted
	Outgoing EMS
	Outgoing EMS - Deleted
MMS Messages	
	Incoming Audio
	Incoming Image
	Incoming Video
	Outgoing Audio
	Outgoing Image
	Outgoing Video
Stand-alone data files	
	Audio
	Audio - Deleted
	Image
	Image - Deleted
	Video
	Video - Deleted

Log	Created By .XRY Version 3.6

Test Case CFT-IMO-01 Micro Systemation .XRY Version 3.6	
Highlights:	Acquisition started: Fri Apr 11 12:18:47 EDT 2008 Acquisition finished: Fri Apr 11 12:23:23 EDT 2008 Acquisition finished: Fri Apr 11 12:27:57 EDT 2008 Complete representation of known data via generated reports was successful
Results:	

Assertion & Expected Result	Actual Result
A_IMO-38 Comparison of known device data elements via generated reports.	as expected

Analysis:	Expected results achieved

5.2.49   CFT-IMO-02   (Motorola RAZR V3)

Test Case CFT-IMO-02 Micro Systemation .XRY Version 3.6	
Case Summary:	CFT-IMO-02 Acquire mobile device internal memory and review reported data via the preview-pane.
Assertions:	A_IMO-39 If a cellular forensic tool successfully completes acquisition of the target device then the tool shall present the acquired data without modification in a preview-pane view.
Tester Name:	rpa
Test Host:	Morrisy
Test Date:	Fri Apr 11 12:26:06 EDT 2008
Device:	Motorola RAZR V3
Source Setup:	OS: WIN XP Interface: cable

DATA OBJECTS	DATA ELEMENTS
Address Book Entries	
	Maximum Length
	Regular Length, email, picture
	Special Character
	Blank Name
	Regular Length, Deleted email - deleted picture
	Deleted Entry
	Foreign Entry
PIM Data	
	Maximum Length
	Regular Length
	Deleted Entry
	Special Character
Call Logs	
	Missed
	Missed - Deleted
	Incoming
	Incoming - Deleted
	Outgoing
	Outgoing - Deleted
Text Messages	
	Incoming SMS - Read
	Incoming SMS - Unread
	Incoming SMS - Deleted
	Outgoing SMS
	Outgoing SMS - Deleted
	Incoming EMS - Read
	Incoming EMS - Unread
	Incoming Foreign EMS - Read
	Incoming EMS - Deleted
	Outgoing EMS
	Outgoing EMS - Deleted
MMS Messages	
	Incoming Audio
	Incoming Image
	Incoming Video
	Outgoing Audio
	Outgoing Image
	Outgoing Video
Stand-alone data files	
	Audio
	Audio - Deleted
	Image
	Image - Deleted
	Video
	Video - Deleted

Log	Created By .XRY Version 3.6

Test Case CFT-IMO-02 Micro Systemation .XRY Version 3.6		
Highlights:	Acquisition started: Fri Apr 11 12:26:06 EDT 2008 Complete representation of known data via preview-pane was successful	
Results:	**Assertion & Expected Result**	**Actual Result**
	A_IMO-39 Comparison of known device data elements via preview-pane.	as expected
Analysis:	Expected results achieved	

5.2.50   CFT-IMO-03   (Motorola RAZR V3)

Test Case CFT-IMO-03 Micro Systemation .XRY Version 3.6	
Case Summary:	CFT-IMO-03 Acquire mobile device internal memory and compare reported data via the preview-pane and supported generated reports.
Assertions:	A_IMO-38 If a cellular forensic tool successfully completes acquisition of the target device then the tool shall present the acquired data without modification via supported generated report formats. A_IMO-39 If a cellular forensic tool successfully completes acquisition of the target device then the tool shall present the acquired data without modification in a preview-pane view. A_IMO-40 If a cellular forensic tool provides a preview-pane view and a generated report of the acquired data then the reports shall maintain consistency of all reported data elements.
Tester Name:	rpa
Test Host:	Morrisy
Test Date:	Fri Apr 11 12:28:54 EDT 2008
Device:	Motorola_RAZR_V3

Source Setup:	OS: WIN XP Interface: cable	

DATA OBJECTS	DATA ELEMENTS
Address Book Entries	
	Maximum Length
	Regular Length, email, picture
	Special Character
	Blank Name
	Regular Length, Deleted email - deleted picture
	Deleted Entry
	Foreign Entry
PIM Data	
	Maximum Length
	Regular Length
	Deleted Entry
	Special Character
Call Logs	
	Missed
	Missed - Deleted
	Incoming
	Incoming - Deleted
	Outgoing
	Outgoing - Deleted
Text Messages	
	Incoming SMS - Read
	Incoming SMS - Unread
	Incoming SMS - Deleted
	Outgoing SMS
	Outgoing SMS - Deleted
	Incoming EMS - Read
	Incoming EMS - Unread
	Incoming Foreign EMS - Read
	Incoming EMS - Deleted
	Outgoing EMS
	Outgoing EMS - Deleted
MMS Messages	
	Incoming Audio
	Incoming Image
	Incoming Video
	Outgoing Audio
	Outgoing Image
	Outgoing Video
Stand-alone data files	
	Audio
	Audio - Deleted
	Image
	Image - Deleted
	Video

Test Case CFT-IMO-03 Micro Systemation .XRY Version 3.6		
	Video - Deleted	
Log Highlights:	Created By .XRY Version 3.6 Acquisition started: Fri Apr 11 12:28:54 EDT 2008 Acquisition finished: Fri Apr 11 12:30:47 EDT 2008 Complete representation of known data via generated reports was successful Complete representation of known data via preview-pane was successful Consistency between generated reports and preview-pane was successful	
Results:		

Assertion & Expected Result	Actual Result
A_IMO-38 Comparison of known device data elements via generated reports.	as expected
A_IMO-39 Comparison of known device data elements via preview-pane.	as expected
A_IMO-40 Compare generated reports and preview-pane views for device acquisition.	as expected

Analysis:	Expected results achieved

5.2.51　　CFT-IMO-04　　(Motorola RAZR V3)

Test Case CFT-IMO-04 Micro Systemation .XRY Version 3.6	
Case Summary:	CFT-IMO-04 After a successful mobile device internal memory acquisition, alter the case file via third party means and attempt to re-open the case.
Assertions:	A_IMO-41 If modification is attempted to the case file or individual data elements via third-party means then the tool shall provide protection mechanisms disallowing or reporting data modification.
Tester Name:	rpa
Test Host:	Morrisy
Test Date:	Fri Apr 11 12:31:21 EDT 2008
Device:	Motorola RAZR V3
Source Setup:	OS: WIN XP Interface: cable

DATA OBJECTS	DATA ELEMENTS
Address Book Entries	
	Maximum Length
	Regular Length, email, picture
	Special Character
	Blank Name
	Regular Length, Deleted email - deleted picture
	Deleted Entry
	Foreign Entry
PIM Data	
	Maximum Length
	Regular Length
	Deleted Entry
	Special Character
Call Logs	
	Missed
	Missed　- Deleted
	Incoming
	Incoming - Deleted
	Outgoing
	Outgoing - Deleted
Text Messages	
	Incoming SMS - Read
	Incoming SMS - Unread
	Incoming SMS - Deleted
	Outgoing SMS
	Outgoing SMS - Deleted
	Incoming EMS - Read
	Incoming EMS - Unread
	Incoming Foreign EMS - Read
	Incoming EMS - Deleted
	Outgoing EMS
	Outgoing EMS - Deleted
MMS Messages	
	Incoming Audio
	Incoming Image
	Incoming Video
	Outgoing Audio
	Outgoing Image
	Outgoing Video
Stand-alone data files	
	Audio
	Audio - Deleted
	Image
	Image - Deleted
	Video
	Video - Deleted

Log	Created By .XRY Version 3.6

Test Case CFT-IMO-04 Micro Systemation .XRY Version 3.6	
Highlights:	Acquisition started: Fri Apr 11 12:31:21 EDT 2008 Acquisition finished: Fri Apr 11 12:34:34 EDT 2008 Notification of modified case data was successful **Notes:** Case File Encryption has to be selected before Acquisition
Results:	

Assertion & Expected Result	Actual Result
A_IMO-41 Notification of modified device case data.	as expected

Analysis:	Expected results achieved

5.2.52   CFT-IMO-07   (Motorola RAZR V3)

Test Case CFT-IMO-07 Micro Systemation .XRY Version 3.6	
Case Summary:	CFT-IMO-07 Create a SIM access card via vendor documentation.
Assertions:	A_IMO-51 If the cellular forensic tool supports SIM access card creation then the card creation shall be completed without errors via manufacturer suggested protocols. Access cards characteristics should be consistent with vendor documentation.
Tester Name:	rpa
Test Host:	Morrisy
Test Date:	Fri Apr 11 12:38:51 EDT 2008
Device:	ATT SIM
Source Setup:	OS: WIN XP Interface: USB

DATA OBJECTS	DATA ELEMENTS
Address Book Entries	
	Maximum Length
	Regular Length, email, picture
	Special Character
	Blank Name
	Regular Length, Deleted email - deleted picture
	Deleted Entry
	Foreign Entry
PIM Data	
	Maximum Length
	Regular Length
	Deleted Entry
	Special Character
Call Logs	
	Missed
	Missed - Deleted
	Incoming
	Incoming - Deleted
	Outgoing
	Outgoing - Deleted
Text Messages	
	Incoming SMS - Read
	Incoming SMS - Unread
	Incoming SMS - Deleted
	Outgoing SMS
	Outgoing SMS - Deleted
	Incoming EMS - Read
	Incoming EMS - Unread
	Incoming Foreign EMS - Read
	Incoming EMS - Deleted
	Outgoing EMS
	Outgoing EMS - Deleted
MMS Messages	
	Incoming Audio
	Incoming Image
	Incoming Video
	Outgoing Audio
	Outgoing Image
	Outgoing Video
Stand-alone data files	
	Audio
	Audio - Deleted
	Image
	Image - Deleted
	Video
	Video - Deleted

Test Case CFT-IMO-07 Micro Systemation .XRY Version 3.6	
Log Highlights:	Created By .XRY Version 3.6 Acquisition started: Fri Apr 11 12:38:51 EDT 2008 Acquisition finished: Fri Apr 11 12:44:25 EDT 2008 Access card creation was successful
Results:	
	<table><tr><td>**Assertion & Expected Result**</td><td>**Actual Result**</td></tr><tr><td>A IMO-51 Access card creation.</td><td>as expected</td></tr></table>
Analysis:	Expected results achieved

5.2.53   CFT-IMO-08   (Motorola RAZR V3)

Test Case CFT-IMO-08 Micro Systemation .XRY Version 3.6	
Case Summary:	CFT-IMO-08 Acquire mobile device internal memory and review generated log files.
Assertions:	A_IMO-52 If the cellular forensic tool supports log creation then the application should present the log files outlining the acquisition process in a human-readable format.
Tester Name:	rpa
Test Host:	Morrisy
Test Date:	Fri Apr 11 12:45:36 EDT 2008
Device:	Motorola RAZR V3
Source Setup:	OS: WIN XP Interface: cable

DATA OBJECTS	DATA ELEMENTS
Address Book Entries	
	Maximum Length
	Regular Length, email, picture
	Special Character
	Blank Name
	Regular Length, Deleted email - deleted picture
	Deleted Entry
	Foreign Entry
PIM Data	
	Maximum Length
	Regular Length
	Deleted Entry
	Special Character
Call Logs	
	Missed
	Missed - Deleted
	Incoming
	Incoming - Deleted
	Outgoing
	Outgoing - Deleted
Text Messages	
	Incoming SMS - Read
	Incoming SMS - Unread
	Incoming SMS - Deleted
	Outgoing SMS
	Outgoing SMS - Deleted
	Incoming EMS - Read
	Incoming EMS - Unread
	Incoming Foreign EMS - Read
	Incoming EMS - Deleted
	Outgoing EMS
	Outgoing EMS - Deleted
MMS Messages	
	Incoming Audio
	Incoming Image
	Incoming Video
	Outgoing Audio
	Outgoing Image
	Outgoing Video
Stand-alone data files	
	Audio
	Audio - Deleted
	Image
	Image - Deleted
	Video
	Video - Deleted

```
Test Case CFT-IMO-08 Micro Systemation .XRY Version 3.6
```

Log	Created By .XRY Version 3.6
Highlights:	Acquisition started: Fri Apr 11 12:45:36 EDT 2008
	Acquisition finished: Fri Apr 11 12:48:41 EDT 2008

```
                Creation of complete and human-readable log files was successful

                Notes:

                XRY Log

                Module          Status          Message
                ------          -------         -------
                MAIN            Success         Initiating Process
                MAIN            Success         .XRY Version 3.6
                MAIN            Success         Connected to Motorola USB Modem #3 [COM11]
                MAIN            Success         Device Name: Motorola V3
                MAIN            Success         CGMI Resp = [+CGMI: "Motorola CE, Copyright
                2004"]
                MAIN            Success         CGMM Resp = [+CGMM:
                "GSM900","GSM1800","GSM1900","GSM850","MODEL=V3re"]
                MAIN            Success         CGMR Resp = [+CGMR: "R3442A_G_0E.43.08R"]
                MAIN            Success         I3 Resp = [Motorola Mobile Phone]
                MAIN            Success         Starting process of GSM0707 (3.5)
                GSM0707         Success         Connecting
                GSM0707         Success         Analyzing General Information
                GSM0707         Success         Reading General Information
                GSM0707         Success         Disconnecting
                MAIN            Success         GSM0707 (3.5) completed successfully
                MAIN            Success         Starting process of Motorola (3.5)
                MOTOROLA        Success         Connecting
                MOTOROLA        Success         Analyzing Contacts
                MOTOROLA        Success         Reading Contacts ME
                MOTOROLA        Success         Reading Contacts SM
                MOTOROLA        Success         Analyzing Calls
                MOTOROLA        Success         Reading Calls DC
                MOTOROLA        Success         Reading Calls MC
                MOTOROLA        Success         Reading Calls RC
                MOTOROLA        Success         Analyzing Calendar
                MOTOROLA        Success         Reading Calendar
                MOTOROLA        Success         Analyzing SMS
                MOTOROLA        Success         Reading SMS IM (6 items)
                MOTOROLA        Success         Disconnecting
                MAIN            Success         Motorola (3.5) completed successfully
                MAIN            Success         Starting process of OBEX (3.5)
                OBEX            Success         Connecting
                OBEX            Success         Connecting OBEX
                OBEX            Success         Analyzing
                OBEX            Success         Analyzing audio
                OBEX            Success         Reading chare.wav
                OBEX            Success         Reading french.mp3
                OBEX            Success         Analyzing video
                OBEX            Success         Reading 11-30-07_1038.3gp
                OBEX            Success         Reading 11-30-07_0954.3gp
                OBEX            Success         Reading 11-30-07_1037.3gp
                OBEX            Success         Analyzing picture
                OBEX            Success         Reading emma-girl.jpg
                OBEX            Success         Reading 11-28-07_1330.jpg
                OBEX            Success         Reading 11-30-07_0856.jpg
                OBEX            Success         Reading Sunset.jpg
                OBEX            Success         Reading 11-28-07_1335.jpg
                OBEX            Success         Disconnecting OBEX
                OBEX            Success         Disconnecting
                MAIN            Success         OBEX (3.5) completed successfully
                MAIN            Success         Processing completed successfully.
                MAIN            Success         Total processing time: 0 minutes, 59 seconds
                MAIN            Success         11 items read to General Information folder
                MAIN            Success         14 items read to Contacts folder
                MAIN            Success         1 items read to Calendar folder
                MAIN            Success         6 items read to SMS folder
                MAIN            Success         5 items read to Pictures folder
```

Test Case CFT-IMO-08 Micro Systemation .XRY Version 3.6			
	MAIN	Success	3 items read to Videos folder
	MAIN	Success	2 items read to Audio folder

Results:		
	Assertion & Expected Result	**Actual Result**
	A IMO-52 Device Log file output.	as expected

Analysis:	Expected results achieved

5.2.54 CFT-IMO-09 (Motorola RAZR V3)

Test Case CFT-IMO-09 Micro Systemation .XRY Version 3.6	
Case Summary:	CFT-IMO-09 Acquire mobile device internal memory and review data containing foreign language characters.
Assertions:	A_IMO-38 If a cellular forensic tool successfully completes acquisition of the target device then the tool shall present the acquired data without modification via supported generated report formats. A_IMO-39 If a cellular forensic tool successfully completes acquisition of the target device then the tool shall present the acquired data without modification in a preview-pane view. A_IMO-53 If the cellular forensic tool supports proper display of foreign language character sets then the application should present address book entries containing foreign language characters in their native format without modification. A_IMO-54 If the cellular forensic tool supports proper display of foreign language character sets then the application should present text messages containing foreign language characters in their native format without modification.
Tester Name:	rpa
Test Host:	Morrisy
Test Date:	Fri Apr 11 12:51:57 EDT 2008
Device:	Motorola_RAZR_V3
Source Setup:	OS: WIN XP Interface: cable

DATA OBJECTS	DATA ELEMENTS
Address Book Entries	
	Maximum Length
	Regular Length, email, picture
	Special Character
	Blank Name
	Regular Length, Deleted email - deleted picture
	Deleted Entry
	Foreign Entry
PIM Data	
	Maximum Length
	Regular Length
	Deleted Entry
	Special Character
Call Logs	
	Missed
	Missed - Deleted
	Incoming
	Incoming - Deleted
	Outgoing
	Outgoing - Deleted
Text Messages	
	Incoming SMS - Read
	Incoming SMS - Unread
	Incoming SMS - Deleted
	Outgoing SMS
	Outgoing SMS - Deleted
	Incoming EMS - Read
	Incoming EMS - Unread
	Incoming Foreign EMS - Read
	Incoming EMS - Deleted
	Outgoing EMS
	Outgoing EMS - Deleted
MMS Messages	
	Incoming Audio
	Incoming Image
	Incoming Video
	Outgoing Audio
	Outgoing Image
	Outgoing Video

Test Case CFT-IMO-09 Micro Systemation .XRY Version 3.6		
	Stand-alone data files	
		Audio
		Audio - Deleted
		Image
		Image - Deleted
		Video
		Video - Deleted

Log Highlights:	Created By .XRY Version 3.6 Acquisition started: Fri Apr 11 12:51:57 EDT 2008 Acquisition finished: Fri Apr 11 12:54:20 EDT 2008 Complete representation of known data via generated reports was successful Complete representation of known data via preview-pane was successful Foreign character Address book entries were acquired and properly displayed Foreign character text messages were acquired and properly displayed

Results:		

Assertion & Expected Result	Actual Result
A_IMO-38 Comparison of known device data elements via generated reports.	as expected
A_IMO-39 Comparison of known device data elements via preview-pane.	as expected
A_IMO-53 Acquisition of address book entries containing foreign language characters.	as expected
A_IMO-54 Acquisition of outgoing text messages containing foreign language characters.	as expected

Analysis:	Expected results achieved

5.2.55   CFT-IMO-11   (Motorola RAZR V3)

Test Case CFT-IMO-11 Micro Systemation .XRY Version 3.6	
Case Summary:	CFT-IMO-11 Acquire mobile device internal memory and review hash values for vendor supported data objects.
Assertions:	A_IMO-38 If a cellular forensic tool successfully completes acquisition of the target device then the tool shall present the acquired data without modification via supported generated report formats. A_IMO-39 If a cellular forensic tool successfully completes acquisition of the target device then the tool shall present the acquired data without modification in a preview-pane view. A_IMO-56 If the cellular forensic tool supports hashing for individual data objects then the tool shall present the user with a hash value for each supported data object.
Tester Name:	rpa
Test Host:	Morrisy
Test Date:	Fri Apr 11 12:55:41 EDT 2008
Device:	Motorola RAZR V3
Source Setup:	OS: WIN XP Interface: cable

DATA OBJECTS	DATA ELEMENTS
Address Book Entries	
	Maximum Length
	Regular Length, email, picture
	Special Character
	Blank Name
	Regular Length, Deleted email – deleted picture
	Deleted Entry
	Foreign Entry
PIM Data	
	Maximum Length
	Regular Length
	Deleted Entry
	Special Character
Call Logs	
	Missed
	Missed – Deleted
	Incoming
	Incoming – Deleted
	Outgoing
	Outgoing – Deleted
Text Messages	
	Incoming SMS – Read
	Incoming SMS Unread
	Incoming SMS – Deleted
	Outgoing SMS
	Outgoing SMS – Deleted
	Incoming EMS – Read
	Incoming EMS – Unread
	Incoming Foreign EMS – Read
	Incoming EMS – Deleted
	Outgoing EMS
	Outgoing EMS – Deleted
MMS Messages	
	Incoming Audio
	Incoming Image
	Incoming Video
	Outgoing Audio
	Outgoing Image
	Outgoing Video
Stand-alone data files	
	Audio
	Audio – Deleted
	Image

	Image - Deleted
	Video
	Video - Deleted

Log Highlights:	Created By .XRY Version 3.6 Acquisition started: Fri Apr 11 12:55:41 EDT 2008 Acquisition finished: Fri Apr 11 12:57:58 EDT 2008 Complete representation of known data via generated reports was successful Complete representation of known data via preview-pane was successful Device hash reporting for individual acquired data elements was successful **Notes**: SHA1 and MD5 hashes were successfully calculated for pictures, video, and audio.
Results:	

Assertion & Expected Result	Actual Result
A_IMO-38 Comparison of known device data elements via generated reports.	as expected
A_IMO-39 Comparison of known device data elements via preview-pane.	as expected
A_IMO-56 Device hash reporting for individual acquired data objects.	as expected

Analysis:	Expected results achieved

5.2.56   CFT-SIM-01   (AT&T SIM)

Test Case CFT-SIM-01 Micro Systemation .XRY Version 3.6	
Case Summary:	CFT-SIM-01 Acquire SIM over supported interfaces (e.g., PC/SC reader, proprietary reader).
Assertions:	A_SIM-23 If a cellular forensic tool provides support for connectivity of the target SIM then the tool shall successfully recognize the target SIM via all vendor supported interfaces (e.g., PC/SC reader, proprietary reader).
Tester Name:	rpa
Test Host:	Morrisy
Test Date:	Thu Apr 3 14:01:20 EDT 2008
Device:	ATT SIM
Source Setup:	OS: WIN XP Interface: USB

DATA OBJECTS	DATA ELEMENTS
Abbreviated Dialing Numbers (ADN)	
	Maximum Length
	Special Character
	Blank Name
	Regular Length - Deleted Number
	Foreign Entry
Call Logs	
	Last Numbers Dialed (LND)
Text Messages	
	Incoming SMS - Read
	Incoming SMS - Foreign
	Incoming SMS - Deleted
	Incoming SMS - Unread
	Incoming Foreign EMS - Read
	Incoming EMS - Deleted

Log Highlights:	Created By .XRY Version 3.6 Acquisition started: Thu Apr 3 14:01:20 EDT 2008 Acquisition finished: Thu Apr 3 14:05:39 EDT 2008 Media connectivity was established via supported interface

Results:		
	Assertion & Expected Result	**Actual Result**
	A_SIM-23 SIM connectivity via supported interfaces.	as expected

Analysis:	Expected results achieved

5.2.57   CFT-SIM-02   (AT&T SIM)

Test Case CFT-SIM-02 Micro Systemation .XRY Version 3.6	
Case Summary:	CFT-SIM-02 Attempt acquisition of a non-supported SIM.
Assertions:	A_SIM-24 If a cellular forensic tool attempts to connect to a non-supported SIM then the tool shall have the ability to identify that the SIM is not supported.
Tester Name:	rpa
Test Host:	Morrisy
Test Date:	Thu Apr 3 14:07:09 EDT 2008
Device:	ATT SIM
Source Setup:	OS: WIN XP Interface: USB

DATA OBJECTS	DATA ELEMENTS
Abbreviated Dialing Numbers (ADN)	
	Maximum Length
	Special Character
	Blank Name
	Regular Length - Deleted Number
	Foreign Entry
Call Logs	
	Last Numbers Dialed (LND)
Text Messages	
	Incoming SMS - Read
	Incoming SMS - Foreign
	Incoming SMS - Deleted
	Incoming SMS - Unread
	Incoming Foreign EMS - Read
	Incoming EMS - Deleted

Log Highlights:	Created By .XRY Version 3.6 Acquisition started: Thu Apr 3 14:07:09 EDT 2008 Acquisition finished: Thu Apr 3 14:08:07 EDT 2008 Identification of non-supported media was successful

Results:		
	Assertion & Expected Result	**Actual Result**
	A_SIM-24 Identification of non-supported SIMs.	as expected

Analysis:	Expected results achieved

5.2.58   CFT-SIM-03   (AT&T SIM)

Test Case CFT-SIM-03 Micro Systemation .XRY Version 3.6	
Case Summary:	CFT-SIM-03 Begin SIM acquisition and interrupt connectivity by interface disengagement.
Assertions:	A_SIM-23 If a cellular forensic tool provides support for connectivity of the target SIM then the tool shall successfully recognize the target SIM via all vendor supported interfaces (e.g., PC/SC reader, proprietary reader). A_SIM-25 If a cellular forensic tool encounters disengagement between the SIM reader and application then the application shall notify the user that connectivity has been disrupted.
Tester Name:	rpa
Test Host:	Morrisy
Test Date:	Thu Apr 3 14:09:03 EDT 2008
Device:	ATT_SIM
Source Setup:	OS: WIN XP Interface: USB

DATA OBJECTS	DATA ELEMENTS
Abbreviated Dialing Numbers (ADN)	
	Maximum Length
	Special Character
	Blank Name
	Regular Length - Deleted Number
	Foreign Entry
Call Logs	
	Last Numbers Dialed (LND)
Text Messages	
	Incoming SMS - Read
	Incoming SMS - Foreign
	Incoming SMS - Deleted
	Incoming SMS - Unread
	Incoming Foreign EMS - Read
	Incoming EMS - Deleted

Log Highlights:	Created By .XRY Version 3.6 Acquisition started: Thu Apr 3 14:09:03 EDT 2008 Acquisition finished: Thu Apr 3 14:10:02 EDT 2008 Media connectivity was established via supported interface Media acquisition disruption notification was successful
Results:	

Assertion & Expected Result	Actual Result
A_SIM-23 SIM connectivity via supported interfaces.	as expected
A_SIM-25 Notification of SIM acquisition disruption.	as expected

Analysis:	Expected results achieved

5.2.59 CFT-SIM-04 (AT&T SIM)

Test Case CFT-SIM-04 Micro Systemation .XRY Version 3.6	
Case Summary:	CFT-SIM-04 Attempt acquisition on a password-protected SIM.
Assertions:	A_SIM-23 If a cellular forensic tool provides support for connectivity of the target SIM then the tool shall successfully recognize the target SIM via all vendor supported interfaces (e.g., PC/SC reader, proprietary reader). A_SIM-26 If the SIM is password-protected then the cellular forensic tool shall provide the examiner with the opportunity to input the PIN before acquisition.
Tester Name:	rpa
Test Host:	Morrisy
Test Date:	Thu Apr 3 14:11:27 EDT 2008
Device:	ATT SIM
Source Setup:	OS: WIN XP Interface: USB

DATA OBJECTS	DATA ELEMENTS
Abbreviated Dialing Numbers (ADN)	
	Maximum Length
	Special Character
	Blank Name
	Regular Length - Deleted Number
	Foreign Entry
Call Logs	
	Last Numbers Dialed (LND)
Text Messages	
	Incoming SMS - Read
	Incoming SMS - Foreign
	Incoming SMS - Deleted
	Incoming SMS - Unread
	Incoming Foreign EMS - Read
	Incoming EMS - Deleted

Log Highlights:	Created By .XRY Version 3.6 Acquisition started: Thu Apr 3 14:11:27 EDT 2008 Acquisition finished: Thu Apr 3 14:12:25 EDT 2008 Media connectivity was established via supported interface Ability to enter PIN on protected media before acquisition was successful
Results:	

Assertion & Expected Result	Actual Result
A_SIM-23 SIM connectivity via supported interfaces.	as expected
A_SIM-26 Password entry before acquisition for protected SIMs.	as expected

Analysis:	Expected results achieved

5.2.60   CFT-SIM-05   (AT&T SIM)

Test Case CFT-SIM-05 Micro Systemation .XRY Version 3.6	
Case Summary:	CFT-SIM-05 Acquire SIM internal memory and review reported data via the preview-pane or generated reports for readability.
Assertions:	A_SIM-23 If a cellular forensic tool provides support for connectivity of the target SIM then the tool shall successfully recognize the target SIM via all vendor supported interfaces (e.g., PC/SC reader, proprietary reader). A_SIM-27 If a cellular forensic tool successfully completes acquisition of the target SIM then the tool shall have the ability to present acquired data in a human-readable format via either preview-pane or generated report.
Tester Name:	rpa
Test Host:	Morrisy
Test Date:	Thu Apr 3 14:13:14 EDT 2008
Device:	ATT_SIM
Source Setup:	OS: WIN XP Interface: USB

DATA OBJECTS	DATA ELEMENTS
Abbreviated Dialing Numbers (ADN)	
	Maximum Length
	Special Character
	Blank Name
	Regular Length - Deleted Number
	Foreign Entry
Call Logs	
	Last Numbers Dialed (LND)
Text Messages	
	Incoming SMS - Read
	Incoming SMS - Foreign
	Incoming SMS - Deleted
	Incoming SMS - Unread
	Incoming Foreign EMS - Read
	Incoming EMS - Deleted

Log Highlights:	Created By .XRY Version 3.6 Acquisition started: Thu Apr 3 14:13:14 EDT 2008 Acquisition finished: Thu Apr 3 14:14:35 EDT 2008 Media connectivity was established via supported interface Readability and completeness of acquired data was successful
Results:	

Assertion & Expected Result	Actual Result
A_SIM-23 SIM connectivity via supported interfaces.	as expected
A_SIM-27 Readability and completeness of acquired data via supported reports.	as expected

Analysis:	Expected results achieved

5.2.61   CFT-SIM-06   (AT&T SIM)

Test Case CFT-SIM-06 Micro Systemation .XRY Version 3.6	
Case Summary:	CFT-SIM-06 Acquire SIM internal memory and review reported subscriber and equipment related information (i.e., SPN, ICCID, IMSI, MSISDN).
Assertions:	A_SIM-23 If a cellular forensic tool provides support for connectivity of the target SIM then the tool shall successfully recognize the target SIM via all vendor supported interfaces (e.g., PC/SC reader, proprietary reader). A_SIM-27 If a cellular forensic tool successfully completes acquisition of the target SIM then the tool shall have the ability to present acquired data in a human-readable format via either preview-pane or generated report. A_SIM-28 If a cellular forensic tool successfully completes acquisition of the target SIM then the SPN shall be presented in a human-readable format without modification. A_SIM-29 If a cellular forensic tool successfully completes acquisition of the target SIM then the ICCID shall be presented in a human-readable format without modification. A_SIM-30 If a cellular forensic tool successfully completes acquisition of the target SIM then the IMSI shall be presented in a human-readable format without modification. A_SIM-31 If a cellular forensic tool successfully completes acquisition of the target SIM then the MSISDN shall be presented in a human-readable format without modification.
Tester Name:	rpa
Test Host:	Morrisy
Test Date:	Thu Apr 3 14:16:10 EDT 2008
Device:	ATT SIM
Source Setup:	OS: WIN XP Interface: USB

DATA OBJECTS	DATA ELEMENTS
Abbreviated Dialing Numbers (ADN)	
	Maximum Length
	Special Character
	Blank Name
	Regular Length - Deleted Number
	Foreign Entry
Call Logs	
	Last Numbers Dialed (LND)
Text Messages	
	Incoming SMS - Read
	Incoming SMS - Foreign
	Incoming SMS - Deleted
	Incoming SMS - Unread
	Incoming Foreign EMS - Read
	Incoming EMS - Deleted

Log Highlights:	Created By .XRY Version 3.6 Acquisition started: Thu Apr 3 14:16:10 EDT 2008 Acquisition finished: Thu Apr 3 14:17:40 EDT 2008 Media connectivity was established via supported interface Readability and completeness of acquired data was successful All subscriber-related data (i.e., SPN, ICCID, IMSI, MSISDN) was acquired
Results:	

Assertion & Expected Result	Actual Result
A_SIM-23 SIM connectivity via supported interfaces.	as expected
A_SIM-27 Readability and completeness of acquired data via supported reports.	as expected
A_SIM-28 Acquisition of SPN.	as expected
A_SIM-29 Acquisition of ICCID.	as expected
A_SIM-30 Acquisition of IMSI.	as expected

Test Case CFT-SIM-06 Micro Systemation .XRY Version 3.6		
	A SIM-31 Acquisition of MSISDN.	as expected
Analysis:	Expected results achieved	

5.2.62 CFT-SIM-07 (AT&T SIM)

Test Case CFT-SIM-07 Micro Systemation .XRY Version 3.6	
Case Summary:	CFT-SIM-07 Acquire SIM internal memory and review reported Abbreviated Dialing Numbers (ADNs).
Assertions:	A_SIM-23 If a cellular forensic tool provides support for connectivity of the target SIM then the tool shall successfully recognize the target SIM via all vendor supported interfaces (e.g., PC/SC reader, proprietary reader). A_SIM-27 If a cellular forensic tool successfully completes acquisition of the target SIM then the tool shall have the ability to present acquired data in a human-readable format via either preview-pane or generated report. A_SIM-32 If a cellular forensic tool successfully completes acquisition of the target SIM then all Abbreviated Dialing Numbers (ADN) shall be presented in a human-readable format without modification.
Tester Name:	rpa
Test Host:	Morrisy
Test Date:	Thu Apr 3 14:18:32 EDT 2008
Device:	ATT SIM
Source Setup:	OS: WIN XP Interface: USB

DATA OBJECTS	DATA ELEMENTS
Abbreviated Dialing Numbers (ADN)	
	Maximum Length
	Special Character
	Blank Name
	Regular Length - Deleted Number
	Foreign Entry
Call Logs	
	Last Numbers Dialed (LND)
Text Messages	
	Incoming SMS - Read
	Incoming SMS - Foreign
	Incoming SMS - Deleted
	Incoming SMS - Unread
	Incoming Foreign EMS - Read
	Incoming EMS - Deleted

Log Highlights:	Created By .XRY Version 3.6 Acquisition started: Thu Apr 3 14:18:32 EDT 2008 Acquisition finished: Thu Apr 3 14:20:08 EDT 2008 Media connectivity was established via supported interface Readability and completeness of acquired data was successful All ADNs were acquired

Results:	

Assertion & Expected Result	Actual Result
A_SIM-23 SIM connectivity via supported interfaces.	as expected
A_SIM-27 Readability and completeness of acquired data via supported reports.	as expected
A_SIM-32 Acquisition of ADNs.	as expected

Analysis:	Expected results achieved

5.2.63 CFT-SIM-08 (AT&T SIM)

Test Case CFT-SIM-08 Micro Systemation .XRY Version 3.6	
Case Summary:	CFT-SIM-08 Acquire SIM internal memory and review reported Last Numbers Dialed (LND).
Assertions:	A_SIM-23 If a cellular forensic tool provides support for connectivity of the target SIM then the tool shall successfully recognize the target SIM via all vendor supported interfaces (e.g., PC/SC reader, proprietary reader). A_SIM-27 If a cellular forensic tool successfully completes acquisition of the target SIM then the tool shall have the ability to present acquired data in a human-readable format via either preview-pane or generated report. A_SIM-33 If a cellular forensic tool successfully completes acquisition of the target SIM then all Last Numbers Dialed (LND) shall be presented in a human-readable format without modification.
Tester Name:	rpa
Test Host:	Morrisy
Test Date:	Thu Apr 3 14:20:59 EDT 2008
Device:	ATT SIM
Source Setup:	OS: WIN XP Interface: USB

DATA OBJECTS	DATA ELEMENTS
Abbreviated Dialing Numbers (ADN)	
	Maximum Length
	Special Character
	Blank Name
	Regular Length - Deleted Number
	Foreign Entry
Call Logs	
	Last Numbers Dialed (LND)
Text Messages	
	Incoming SMS - Read
	Incoming SMS - Foreign
	Incoming SMS - Deleted
	Incoming SMS - Unread
	Incoming Foreign EMS - Read
	Incoming EMS - Deleted

Log Highlights:	Created By .XRY Version 3.6 Acquisition started: Thu Apr 3 14:20:59 EDT 2008 Acquisition finished: Thu Apr 3 14:23:22 EDT 2008 Media connectivity was established via supported interface Readability and completeness of acquired data was successful LNDs were acquired

Results:		
Assertion & Expected Result		**Actual Result**
A_SIM-23 SIM connectivity via supported interfaces.		as expected
A_SIM-27 Readability and completeness of acquired data via supported reports.		as expected
A_SIM-33 Acquisition of LNDs.		as expected

Analysis:	Expected results achieved

5.2.64　　CFT-SIM-09　　(AT&T SIM)

Test Case CFT-SIM-09 Micro Systemation .XRY Version 3.6	
Case Summary:	CFT-SIM-09 Acquire SIM internal memory and review reported text messages (i.e., SMS, EMS).
Assertions:	A_SIM-23 If a cellular forensic tool provides support for connectivity of the target SIM then the tool shall successfully recognize the target SIM via all vendor supported interfaces (e.g., PC/SC reader, proprietary reader). A_SIM-27 If a cellular forensic tool successfully completes acquisition of the target SIM then the tool shall have the ability to present acquired data in a human-readable format via either preview-pane or generated report. A_SIM-34 If a cellular forensic tool successfully completes acquisition of the target SIM then all SMS text messages shall be presented in a human-readable format without modification. A_SIM-35 If a cellular forensic tool successfully completes acquisition of the target SIM then all EMS text messages shall be presented in a human-readable format without modification.
Tester Name:	rpa
Test Host:	Morrisy
Test Date:	Thu Apr 3 14:24:12 EDT 2008
Device:	ATT_SIM
Source Setup:	OS: WIN XP Interface: USB

DATA OBJECTS	DATA ELEMENTS
Abbreviated Dialing Numbers (ADN)	
	Maximum Length
	Special Character
	Blank Name
	Regular Length - Deleted Number
	Foreign Entry
Call Logs	
	Last Numbers Dialed (LND)
Text Messages	
	Incoming SMS - Read
	Incoming SMS - Foreign
	Incoming SMS - Deleted
	Incoming SMS - Unread
	Incoming Foreign EMS - Read
	Incoming EMS - Deleted

Log Highlights:	Created By .XRY Version 3.6 Acquisition started: Thu Apr 3 14:24:12 EDT 2008 Acquisition finished: Thu Apr 3 14:25:30 EDT 2008 Media connectivity was established via supported interface Readability and completeness of acquired data was successful ALL text messages (SMS, EMS) were acquired

Results:	Assertion & Expected Result	Actual Result
	A_SIM-23 SIM connectivity via supported interfaces.	as expected
	A_SIM-27 Readability and completeness of acquired data via supported reports.	as expected
	A_SIM-34 Acquisition of SMS messages.	as expected
	A_SIM-35 Acquisition of EMS messages.	as expected

Analysis:	Expected results achieved

5.2.65   CFT-SIM-10   (AT&T SIM)

Test Case CFT-SIM-10 Micro Systemation .XRY Version 3.6	
Case Summary:	CFT-SIM-10 Acquire SIM internal memory and review reported location related data (i.e., LOCI, GPRSLOCI).
Assertions:	A_SIM-23 If a cellular forensic tool provides support for connectivity of the target SIM then the tool shall successfully recognize the target SIM via all vendor supported interfaces (e.g., PC/SC reader, proprietary reader). A_SIM-27 If a cellular forensic tool successfully completes acquisition of the target SIM then the tool shall have the ability to present acquired data in a human-readable format via either preview-pane or generated report. A_SIM-36 If a cellular forensic tool successfully completes acquisition of the target SIM then all location related data (i.e., LOCI) shall be presented in a human-readable format without modification. A_SIM-37 If a cellular forensic tool successfully completes acquisition of the target SIM then all location related data (i.e., GRPSLOCI) shall be presented in a human-readable format without modification.
Tester Name:	rpa
Test Host:	Morrisy
Test Date:	Thu Apr 3 14:26:05 EDT 2008
Device:	ATT SIM
Source Setup:	OS: WIN XP Interface: USB

DATA OBJECTS	DATA ELEMENTS
Abbreviated Dialing Numbers (ADN)	
	Maximum Length
	Special Character
	Blank Name
	Regular Length - Deleted Number
	Foreign Entry
Call Logs	
	Last Numbers Dialed (LND)
Text Messages	
	Incoming SMS - Read
	Incoming SMS - Foreign
	Incoming SMS - Deleted
	Incoming SMS - Unread
	Incoming Foreign EMS - Read
	Incoming EMS - Deleted

Log Highlights:	Created By .XRY Version 3.6 Acquisition started: Thu Apr 3 14:26:05 EDT 2008 Acquisition finished: Thu Apr 3 14:27:12 EDT 2008 Media connectivity was established via supported interface Readability and completeness of acquired data was successful LOCI data was acquired GPRSLOCI data was acquired

Results:		
	Assertion & Expected Result	**Actual Result**
	A_SIM-23 SIM connectivity via supported interfaces.	as expected
	A_SIM-27 Readability and completeness of acquired data via supported reports.	as expected
	A_SIM-36 Acquisition of LOCI information.	as expected
	A_SIM-37 Acquisition of GPRSLOCI information.	as expected

Analysis:	Expected results achieved

5.2.66   CFT-SIMO-01   (AT&T SIM)

Test Case CFT-SIMO-01 Micro Systemation .XRY Version 3.6	
Case Summary:	CFT-SIMO-01 Acquire SIM internal memory and review acquired data via supported generated report formats.
Assertions:	A_SIMO-58 If a cellular forensic tool successfully completes acquisition of the target media (i.e., SIM) then the tool shall present the acquired data in a human-readable format without modification via supported generated report formats.
Tester Name:	rpa
Test Host:	Morrisy
Test Date:	Fri Apr 4 13:07:02 EDT 2008
Device:	ATT SIM
Source Setup:	OS: WIN XP Interface: USB

DATA OBJECTS	DATA ELEMENTS
Abbreviated Dialing Numbers (ADN)	
	Maximum Length
	Special Character
	Blank Name
	Regular Length - Deleted Number
	Foreign Entry
Call Logs	
	Last Numbers Dialed (LND)
Text Messages	
	Incoming SMS - Read
	Incoming SMS - Foreign
	Incoming SMS - Deleted
	Incoming SMS - Unread
	Incoming Foreign EMS - Read
	Incoming EMS - Deleted

Log Highlights:	Created By .XRY Version 3.6 Acquisition started: Fri Apr 4 13:07:02 EDT 2008 Acquisition finished: Fri Apr 4 13:07:59 EDT 2008 Complete representation of known data via generated reports was successful

Results:		
	Assertion & Expected Result	**Actual Result**
	A_SIMO-58 Comparison of known SIM data elements via generated reports.	as expected

Analysis:	Expected results achieved

5.2.67 CFT-SIMO-02 (AT&T SIM)

Test Case CFT-SIMO-02 Micro Systemation .XRY Version 3.6	
Case Summary:	CFT-SIMO-02 Acquire SIM internal memory and review acquired data via the preview-pane.
Assertions:	A_SIMO-59 If a cellular forensic tool successfully completes acquisition of the target media (i.e., SIM) then the tool shall present the acquired data in a human-readable format without modification via supported generated report formats.
Tester Name:	rpa
Test Host:	Morrisy
Test Date:	Fri Apr 4 13:08:39 EDT 2008
Device:	ATT SIM
Source Setup:	OS: WIN XP Interface: USB

DATA OBJECTS	DATA ELEMENTS
Abbreviated Dialing Numbers (ADN)	
	Maximum Length
	Special Character
	Blank Name
	Regular Length - Deleted Number
	Foreign Entry
Call Logs	
	Last Numbers Dialed (LND)
Text Messages	
	Incoming SMS - Read
	Incoming SMS - Foreign
	Incoming SMS - Deleted
	Incoming SMS - Unread
	Incoming Foreign EMS - Read
	Incoming EMS - Deleted

Log Highlights:	Created By .XRY Version 3.6 Acquisition started: Fri Apr 4 13:08:39 EDT 2008 Acquisition finished: Fri Apr 4 13:09:22 EDT 2008 Complete representation of known data via preview-pane was successful

Results:

Assertion & Expected Result	Actual Result
A SIMO-59 Comparison of known SIM data elements via preview-pane.	as expected

Analysis:	Expected results achieved

5.2.68   CFT-SIMO-03   (AT&T SIM)

Test Case CFT-SIMO-03 Micro Systemation .XRY Version 3.6	
Case Summary:	CFT-SIMO-03 Acquire SIM internal memory and compare acquired data via the preview-pane and supported generated reports.
Assertions:	A_SIMO-58 If a cellular forensic tool successfully completes acquisition of the target media (i.e., SIM) then the tool shall present the acquired data in a human-readable format without modification via supported generated report formats. A_SIMO-59 If a cellular forensic tool successfully completes acquisition of the target media (i.e., SIM) then the tool shall present the acquired data in a human-readable format without modification via supported generated report formats. A_SIMO-60 If a cellular forensic tool provides a preview-pane view and a generated report of the acquired data then the reports shall maintain consistency of all reported data elements.
Tester Name:	rpa
Test Host:	Morrisy
Test Date:	Fri Apr 4 13:09:53 EDT 2008
Device:	ATT SIM
Source Setup:	OS: WIN XP Interface: USB

DATA OBJECTS	DATA ELEMENTS
Abbreviated Dialing Numbers (ADN)	
	Maximum Length
	Special Character
	Blank Name
	Regular Length - Deleted Number
	Foreign Entry
Call Logs	
	Last Numbers Dialed (LND)
Text Messages	
	Incoming SMS - Read
	Incoming SMS - Foreign
	Incoming SMS - Deleted
	Incoming SMS - Unread
	Incoming Foreign EMS - Read
	Incoming EMS - Deleted

Log Highlights:	Created By .XRY Version 3.6 Acquisition started: Fri Apr 4 13:09:53 EDT 2008 Acquisition finished: Fri Apr 4 13:20:51 EDT 2008 Complete representation of known data via generated reports was successful Complete representation of known data via preview-pane was successful

Results:

Assertion & Expected Result	Actual Result
A_SIMO-58 Comparison of known SIM data elements via generated reports.	as expected
A_SIMO-59 Comparison of known SIM data elements via preview-pane.	as expected
A_SIMO-60 Compare generated reports and preview-pane views for SIM acquisition.	as expected

Analysis:	Expected results achieved

5.2.69   CFT-SIMO-04   (AT&T SIM)

Test Case CFT-SIMO-04 Micro Systemation .XRY Version 3.6	
Case Summary:	CFT-SIMO-04 After a successful SIM internal memory acquisition, aflter the case file via third party means and attempt to re-open the case.
Assertions:	A_SIMO-61 If modification is attempted to the case file or individual data elements via third-party means then the tool shall provide protection mechanisms disallowing or reporting data modification.
Tester Name:	rpa
Test Host:	Morrisy
Test Date:	Fri Apr 4 13:37:45 EDT 2008
Device:	ATT_SIM
Source Setup:	OS: WIN XP Interface: USB

DATA OBJECTS	DATA ELEMENTS
Abbreviated Dialing Numbers (ADN)	
	Maximum Length
	Special Character
	Blank Name
	Regular Length - Deleted Number
	Foreign Entry
Call Logs	
	Last Numbers Dialed (LND)
Text Messages	
	Incoming SMS - Read
	Incoming SMS - Foreign
	Incoming SMS - Deleted
	Incoming SMS - Unread
	Incoming Foreign EMS - Read
	Incoming EMS - Deleted

Log Highlights:	Created By .XRY Version 3.6 Acquisition started: Fri Apr 4 13:37:45 EDT 2008 Acquisition finished: Fri Apr 4 13:41:01 EDT 2008 Notification of modified case data was successful **Notes:** Case File Encryption has to be selected before Acquisition
Results:	

Assertion & Expected Result	Actual Result
A_SIMO-61 Notification of modifed SIM case data.	as expected

Analysis:	Expected results achieved

5.2.70   CFT-SIMO-05   (AT&T SIM)

Test Case CFT-SIMO-05 Micro Systemation .XRY Version 3.6	
Case Summary:	CFT-SIMO-05 Acquire SIM internal memory and review reports for recoverable deleted data.
Assertions:	A_SIMO-58 If a cellular forensic tool successfully completes acquisition of the target media (i.e., SIM) then the tool shall present the acquired data in a human-readable format without modification via supported generated report formats. A_SIMO-59 If a cellular forensic tool successfully completes acquisition of the target media (i.e., SIM) then the tool shall present the acquired data in a human-readable format without modification via supported generated report formats. A_SIMO-62 If the cellular forensic tool successfully completes acquisition of the target SIM and recoverable deleted SMS messages exist then the tool shall present recoverable deleted data in a human-readable format without modification. A_SIMO-63 If the cellular forensic tool successfully completes acquisition of the target SIM and recoverable deleted EMS messages exist then the tool shall present recoverable deleted data in a human-readable format without modification.
Tester Name:	rpa
Test Host:	Morrisy
Test Date:	Fri Apr 4 13:44:54 EDT 2008
Device:	ATT SIM
Source Setup:	OS: WIN XP Interface: USB

DATA OBJECTS	DATA ELEMENTS
Abbreviated Dialing Numbers (ADN)	
	Maximum Length
	Special Character
	Blank Name
	Regular Length - Deleted Number
	Foreign Entry
Call Logs	
	Last Numbers Dialed (LND)
Text Messages	
	Incoming SMS - Read
	Incoming SMS - Foreign
	Incoming SMS - Deleted
	Incoming SMS - Unread
	Incoming Foreign EMS - Read
	Incoming EMS - Deleted

Log Highlights:	Created By .XRY Version 3.6 Acquisition started: Fri Apr 4 13:44:54 EDT 2008 Acquisition finished: Fri Apr 4 13:46:28 EDT 2008 Complete representation of known data via generated reports was successful Complete representation of known data via preview-pane was successful Deleted SMS data was recovered Deleted EMS data was recovered

Results:		
	Assertion & Expected Result	**Actual Result**
	A_SIMO-58 Comparison of known SIM data elements via generated reports.	as expected
	A_SIMO-59 Comparison of known SIM data elements via preview-pane.	as expected
	A_SIMO-62 Recovery of deleted SMS messages.	as expected
	A_SIMO-63 Recovery of deleted EMS messages.	as expected

Test Case CFT-SIMO-05 Micro Systemation .XRY Version 3.6	
Analysis:	Expected results achieved

5.2.71 CFT-SIMO-06 (AT&T SIM)

Test Case CFT-SIMO-06 Micro Systemation .XRY Version 3.6	
Case Summary:	CFT-SIMO-06 Acquire SIM internal memory and review generated log files.
Assertions:	A_SIMO-64 If a cellular forensic tool supports creation of log files then the application should present the log files in a human-readable format outlining the acquisition process.
Tester Name:	rpa
Test Host:	Morrisy
Test Date:	Fri Apr 4 13:49:26 EDT 2008
Device:	ATT SIM
Source Setup:	OS: WIN XP Interface: USB

DATA OBJECTS	DATA ELEMENTS
Abbreviated Dialing Numbers (ADN)	
	Maximum Length
	Special Character
	Blank Name
	Regular Length - Deleted Number
	Foreign Entry
Call Logs	
	Last Numbers Dialed (LND)
Text Messages	
	Incoming SMS - Read
	Incoming SMS - Foreign
	Incoming SMS - Deleted
	Incoming SMS - Unread
	Incoming Foreign EMS - Read
	Incoming EMS - Deleted

Log Highlights:	Created By .XRY Version 3.6 Acquisition started: Fri Apr 4 13:49:26 EDT 2008 Acquisition finished: Fri Apr 4 13:51:05 EDT 2008 Creation of complete and human-readable log files was successful **Notes:** XRY Log

Module	Status	Message
------	-------	-------
MAIN	Success	Initiating Process
MAIN	Success	.XRY Version 3.6
MAIN	Success	Connected to OMNIKEY CardMan 6121 0 []
MAIN	Success	Device Name: SIM Card
MAIN	Success	Starting process of SIM (3.6)
SIM	Success	Connecting
SIM	Success	Connected with T0 Protocol
SIM	Success	Detecting SIM type
SIM	Success	Asking user for SIM type
SIM	Success	Identified as SIM Card
SIM	Success	Passed PIN code
SIM	Success	Analyzing MF folder
SIM	Success	Reading General Information
SIM	Success	Reading General Information
SIM	Success	Analyzing GSM Folder
SIM	Success	Reading General Information
SIM	Success	Reading Network Information
SIM	Success	Reading Network Information PLMN Selector
SIM	Success	Reading Network Information Forbidden PLMNs
SIM	Success	Analyzing Telecom Folder
SIM	Success	Reading SMS
SIM	Success	Read 30 positions, 15 used

Test Case CFT-SIMO-06 Micro Systemation .XRY Version 3.6			
	SIM	Success	Reading General Information (MSISDN numbers)
	SIM	Success	Read 4 positions, 1 used
	SIM	Success	Reading Network Information
	SIM	Success	Reading Contacts
	SIM	Success	Read 250 positions, 6 used
	SIM	Success	Reading Contacts (fixed numbers)
	SIM	Success	Read 40 positions, 0 used
	SIM	Success	Reading Contacts (service numbers)
	SIM	Success	Read 5 positions, 0 used
	SIM	Success	Reading Calls (last dialled)
	SIM	Success	Read 10 positions, 4 used
	SIM	Success	Attempting to read 02 IMEI
	SIM	Success	No IMEI Found
	MAIN	Success	SIM (3.6) completed successfully
	MAIN	Success	Processing completed successfully.
	MAIN	Success	Total processing time: 0 minutes, 10 seconds
	MAIN	Success	9 items read to General Information folder
	MAIN	Success	6 items read to Contacts folder
	MAIN	Success	4 items read to Calls folder
	MAIN	Success	8 items read to SMS folder
	MAIN	Success	16 items read to Network Information folder

Results:		
	Assertion & Expected Result	**Actual Result**
	A SIMO-64 SIM log file output.	as expected

Analysis:	Expected results achieved

5.2.72   CFT-SIMO-07   (AT&T SIM)

Test Case CFT-SIMO-07 Micro Systemation .XRY Version 3.6	
Case Summary:	CFT-SIMO-07 Acquire SIM internal memory and review data containing foreign language characters.
Assertions:	A_SIMO-58 If a cellular forensic tool successfully completes acquisition of the target media (i.e., SIM) then the tool shall present the acquired data in a human-readable format without modification via supported generated report formats. A_SIMO-59 If a cellular forensic tool successfully completes acquisition of the target media (i.e., SIM) then the tool shall present the acquired data in a human-readable format without modification via supported generated report formats. A_SIMO-65 If the cellular forensic tool supports proper display of foreign language character sets then the application should present abbreviated dialing numbers (ADNs) containing foreign language characters in their native format without modification. A_SIMO-66 If the cellular forensic tool supports proper display of foreign language character sets then the application should present text messages containing foreign language characters in their native format without modification.
Tester Name:	rpa
Test Host:	Morrisy
Test Date:	Fri Apr 4 13:54:02 EDT 2008
Device:	ATT_SIM
Source Setup:	OS: WIN XP Interface: USB

DATA OBJECTS	DATA ELEMENTS
Abbreviated Dialing Numbers (ADN)	
	Maximum Length
	Special Character
	Blank Name
	Regular Length - Deleted Number
	Foreign Entry
Call Logs	
	Last Numbers Dialed (LND)
Text Messages	
	Incoming SMS - Read
	Incoming SMS - Foreign
	Incoming SMS - Deleted
	Incoming SMS - Unread
	Incoming Foreign EMS - Read
	Incoming EMS - Deleted

Log Highlights:	Created By .XRY Version 3.6 Acquisition started: Fri Apr 4 13:54:02 EDT 2008 Acquisition finished: Fri Apr 4 13:54:55 EDT 2008 Complete representation of known data via generated reports was successful Complete representation of known data via preview-pane was successful ADNs containing foreign characters were acquired and properly displayed Text messages containing foreign characters were acquired and properly displayed

Results:		

Assertion & Expected Result	Actual Result
A_SIMO-58 Comparison of known SIM data elements via generated reports.	as expected
A_SIMO-59 Comparison of known SIM data elements via preview-pane.	as expected
A_SIMO-65 Acquisition of ADNs containing foreign language characters.	as expected
A_SIMO-66 Acquisition of text messages containing foreign	as expected

Test Case CFT-SIMO-07 Micro Systemation .XRY Version 3.6		
	language characters.	
Analysis:	Expected results achieved	

5.2.73   CFT-SIMO-08   (AT&T SIM)

Test Case CFT-SIMO-08 Micro Systemation .XRY Version 3.6	
Case Summary:	CFT-SIMO-08 Begin acquisition on a PIN protected SIM to determine if the tool provides an accurate count of the remaining number of PIN attempts and if the PIN attempts are decremented when entering an incorrect value.
Assertions:	A_SIMO-67 If a cellular forensic tool provides the examiner with the remaining number of authentication attempts then the application should provide an accurate count of the remaining PIN attempts.
Tester Name:	rpa
Test Host:	Morrisy
Test Date:	Fri Apr 4 13:56:00 EDT 2008
Device:	ATT_SIM
Source Setup:	OS: WIN XP Interface: USB

DATA OBJECTS	DATA ELEMENTS
Abbreviated Dialing Numbers (ADN)	
	Maximum Length
	Special Character
	Blank Name
	Regular Length - Deleted Number
	Foreign Entry
Call Logs	
	Last Numbers Dialed (LND)
Text Messages	
	Incoming SMS - Read
	Incoming SMS - Foreign
	Incoming SMS - Deleted
	Incoming SMS - Unread
	Incoming Foreign EMS - Read
	Incoming EMS - Deleted

Log Highlights:	Created By .XRY Version 3.6 Acquisition started: Fri Apr 4 13:56:00 EDT 2008 Acquisition finished: Fri Apr 4 13:57:35 EDT 2008 Remaining number of PIN attempts properly displayed was successful

Results:		
	Assertion & Expected Result	Actual Result
	A_SIMO-67 Display of remaining number of PIN attempts.	as expected

Analysis:	Expected results achieved

5.2.74   CFT-SIMO-09   (AT&T SIM)

Test Case CFT-SIMO-09 Micro Systemation .XRY Version 3.6	
Case Summary:	CFT-SIMO-09 Begin acquisition on a SIM whose PIN attempts have been exhausted to determine if the tool provides an accurate count of the remaining number of PUK attempts and if the PUK attempts are decremented when entering an incorrect value.
Assertions:	A_SIMO-68 If a cellular forensic tool provides the examiner with the remaining number of PUK attempts then the application should provide an accurate count of the remaining PUK attempts.
Tester Name:	rpa
Test Host:	Morrisy
Test Date:	Fri Apr 4 13:59:56 EDT 2008
Device:	ATT_SIM
Source Setup:	OS: WIN XP Interface: USB

DATA OBJECTS	DATA ELEMENTS
Abbreviated Dialing Numbers (ADN)	
	Maximum Length
	Special Character
	Blank Name
	Regular Length - Deleted Number
	Foreign Entry
Call Logs	
	Last Numbers Dialed (LND)
Text Messages	
	Incoming SMS - Read
	Incoming SMS - Foreign
	Incoming SMS - Deleted
	Incoming SMS - Unread
	Incoming Foreign EMS - Read
	Incoming EMS - Deleted

Log Highlights:	Created By .XRY Version 3.6 Acquisition started: Fri Apr 4 13:59:56 EDT 2008 Acquisition finished: Fri Apr 4 14:03:16 EDT 2008 Remaining number of PUK attempts properly displayed was successful

Results:

Assertion & Expected Result	Actual Result
A_SIMO-68 Display of remaining number of PUK attempts.	as expected

Analysis:	Expected results achieved

About the National Institute of Justice

NIJ is the research, development, and evaluation agency of the U.S. Department of Justice. NIJ's mission is to advance scientific research, development, and evaluation to enhance the administration of justice and public safety. NIJ's principal authorities are derived from the Omnibus Crime Control and Safe Streets Act of 1968, as amended (see 42 U.S.C. §§ 3721–3723).

The NIJ Director is appointed by the President and confirmed by the Senate. The Director establishes the Institute's objectives, guided by the priorities of the Office of Justice Programs, the U.S. Department of Justice, and the needs of the field. The Institute actively solicits the views of criminal justice and other professionals and researchers to inform its search for the knowledge and tools to guide policy and practice.

Strategic Goals

NIJ has seven strategic goals grouped into three categories:

Creating relevant knowledge and tools

1. Partner with State and local practitioners and policymakers to identify social science research and technology needs.
2. Create scientific, relevant, and reliable knowledge—with a particular emphasis on terrorism, violent crime, drugs and crime, cost-effectiveness, and community-based efforts—to enhance the administration of justice and public safety.
3. Develop affordable and effective tools and technologies to enhance the administration of justice and public safety.

Dissemination

4. Disseminate relevant knowledge and information to practitioners and policymakers in an understandable, timely, and concise manner.
5. Act as an honest broker to identify the information, tools, and technologies that respond to the needs of stakeholders.

Agency management

6. Practice fairness and openness in the research and development process.
7. Ensure professionalism, excellence, accountability, cost-effectiveness, and integrity in the management and conduct of NIJ activities and programs.

Program Areas

In addressing these strategic challenges, the Institute is involved in the following program areas: crime control and prevention, including policing; drugs and crime; justice systems and offender behavior, including corrections; violence and victimization; communications and information technologies; critical incident response; investigative and forensic sciences, including DNA; less-than-lethal technologies; officer protection; education and training technologies; testing and standards; technology assistance to law enforcement and corrections agencies; field testing of promising programs; and international crime control.

In addition to sponsoring research and development and technology assistance, NIJ evaluates programs, policies, and technologies. NIJ communicates its research and evaluation findings through conferences and print and electronic media.

To find out more about the National Institute of Justice, please visit:

http://www.ojp.usdoj.gov/nij

or contact:

National Criminal Justice
 Reference Service
P.O. Box 6000
Rockville, MD 20849–6000
800–851–3420
http://www.ncjrs.gov

www.ingramcontent.com/pod-product-compliance
Lightning Source LLC
Chambersburg PA
CBHW080255290526
45790CB00005B/1816